Cardinal Zen's Advent Reflections

CARDINAL JOSEPH ZEN

CARDINAL ZEN'S ADVENT REFLECTIONS

Edited by Aurelio Porfiri

Translated by Annie, Reno, Law Wang Tat, and Pauline

SOPHIA INSTITUTE PRESS
Manchester, New Hampshire

Copyright © 2023 by Cardinal Joseph Zen

Printed in the United States of America. All rights reserved.

Cover design by Updatefordesign Studio.

On the cover: Mountain landscape (32461270) © dr. digitex / Freepik.

Unless otherwise noted, Scripture quotations in this book are taken from the Catholic Edition of the Revised Standard Version of the Bible, copyright 1965, 1966 by the Division of Christian Education of the National Council of the Churches of Christ in the United States of America. Used by permission. All rights reserved. Quotations marked "NABRE" are taken from the New American Bible, revised edition © 2010, 1991, 1986, 1970 Confraternity of Christian Doctrine, Washington, D.C. and are used by permission of the copyright owner. All Rights Reserved. No part of the New American Bible may be reproduced in any form without permission in writing from the copyright owner.

No part of this book may be reproduced, stored in a retrieval system, or transmitted in any form, or by any means, electronic, mechanical, photocopying, or otherwise, without the prior written permission of the publisher, except by a reviewer, who may quote brief passages in a review.

Sophia Institute Press
Box 5284, Manchester, NH 03108
1-800-888-9344

www.SophiaInstitute.com

Sophia Institute Press® is a registered trademark of Sophia Institute.

paperback ISBN 979-8-88911-074-3

ebook ISBN 979-8-88911-075-0

Library of Congress Control Number: 2023941853

First printing

Contents

St. John the Baptist and St. Joseph

Jesus the Lord

PART II: CHRISTMAS

A Child Is Born for Us

A Time for Joy

Liturgical Themes

Bringing Salvation to the World

The Mother in the Plan of Salvation

Introduction

by Aurelio Porfiri

Without a doubt, among the most beloved celebrations among Catholics, if not *the* most beloved, is the recurrence of feast of the Birth of the Savior, the celebration of Christmas. We all certainly have memories of this holiday that remind us of many beautiful moments in our families, but we must acknowledge the importance, as well, of the period that precedes Christmas, the season of Advent. Dom Prosper Guéranger, in his admirable comments on the liturgical year, speaks of Advent in these words:

> In the days of Advent, the Savior knocks on the door of every soul, at times perceptibly, at times in a hidden

way. He comes to ask if they have room for him, that he might be born in them. But, although the house he visits is his because he built and preserves it, he complained that his own would not receive him (Jn 1:11), at least the greater number of them. "But to all who received him, who believed in his name, he gave power to become children of God; who were born, not of blood nor of the will of the flesh" (Jn 1:12–13).

Prepare yourselves, therefore, to see Him be born in you more beautiful, more radiant, stronger than you have ever known Him, O faithful souls who bear Him in yourselves like a precious deposit and who have had no other life than His for a long time now, no other heart than His, no other works than His. You know how to gather in from the words of the sacred liturgy those words that evoke your love and that touch the heart of the Bridegroom.

Open the doors to receive Him in His new coming, you who already have Him in you but without knowing Him, who already possessed Him but without savoring Him. He is returning with a new tenderness; He has forgotten your refusal; *He wants to renew all things* (Rev. 21:5). Make room for the celestial Child who wants to grow in you. The moment is near:

> may your heart therefore be aroused; watch and pray that He might not surprise you in sleep when He passes by. The words of the liturgy are also for you because they speak of the darkness that only God can dispel, of wounds that only His goodness can heal, of yearnings that will cease only by means of His virtue.
>
> And you Christians for whom the good news is as if it were not because your hearts have died to sin, whether this death has held you tight in its cords for long years, or whether the wound that it caused was inflicted more recently on your soul, behold coming the One who is life. "Why will you die, O house of Israel? For I have no pleasure in the death of any one, says the Lord GOD; so turn, and live" (Ezek. 18:31–32).
>
> The great celebration of His Birth will be a day of universal mercy for all those who will allow Him to enter. These will begin to live with Him again; every other previous life will be abolished, and *where sin increased, grace abounded all the more* (Rom. 5:20).

These admirable words of the great monk and Benedictine reformer help us to meditate on these liturgical seasons of grace and spiritual fruit.

Christmas finds meaning when we encounter it in the perspective of Advent, which helps us to reflect on the coming in the flesh of the Savior, so as then to reflect on His coming in glory.

Reflecting upon Advent and Christmas with someone like Cardinal Joseph Zen Ze-kiun is quite interesting. Born in Shanghai in 1932, Cardinal Zen was received as an adolescent into the Salesian Fathers to become a son of St. John Bosco. At a certain point, he was transferred to Hong Kong with other students to continue his studies. From there, he was sent to Italy to deepen his academic preparation in Turin and Rome, where he would be able to study philosophy in depth and obtain his doctorate in philosophy. After priestly ordination, he returned to Hong Kong, where he carried out various tasks for his congregation and began to teach. In this regard, the period he taught in seminaries in continental China (from 1989 to 1996) was very important. In 1996, he became coadjutor bishop of Hong Kong and, in 2002, became titular bishop of the diocese. In 2006, he was created a cardinal. He retired as titular bishop in 2009. Even after his retirement, he continues his battles to defend the Church's social teaching.

Many know Cardinal Zen for his public stances in the international media, but it is important to understand that all of this is the fruit not of the strategies of one politically active man but of the aspirations of a man of faith who finds a wellspring of continual inspiration in prayer, especially liturgical prayer. These meditations on Advent and Christmas are the fruit of his spiritual journey at the service of the Church of Hong Kong and of the universal Church. The material for these meditations has been adapted from various sources, including his homilies, discourses, and meditations given especially during his time as bishop of Hong Kong. Cardinal Zen has reviewed the definitive text and added necessary improvements in light of publication.

The hope is that these meditations will help readers to live the liturgical seasons of Advent and Christmas with great fervor and to advance in their life of faith.

Cardinal Zen's Advent Reflections

Part I

ADVENT

A TIME OF PREPARATION

Meditation 1

Time is like a spiral

We would probably agree that the biblical concept of time is not like a circle, which repeats round and round, never having anything new. The biblical concept of time is linear, with a beginning, a process, and an end. In fact, I think it may be more accurate to say that "time is like a spiral" because while there is a cycle year by year, it is not a self-perpetuating circle but one that moves like a spiral toward the goal.

In the final stage of a liturgical year, the Church asks us to meditate on the end times. Now, a new liturgical year also begins with the end times' theme. This connection is manifested in the liturgical arrangement. Advent is divided into two periods: in the beginning, the first period, the liturgy wants us to look forward to the glorious coming of the Savior and then gradually shift our attention to Jesus' coming two thousand years ago. The next period (starting from December 17) is the preparation for the coming Christmas.

Looking forward to the glorious coming of the Savior can be regarded as a "normal task" of the Church after Jesus' Ascension. Being well prepared for Advent is essential, and we believers should always keep that in mind. Of course, it is crucial to cultivate such an eschatological tension.

Meditation 2

Have been and have yet to come

The temple of the Lord upon the high mountain is the home of all nations. The prophet said, "Come, let us go up to the mountain of the LORD, to the house of the God of Jacob" (Isa. 2:3). "I was glad when they said to me, 'Let us go to the house of the Lord!' Our feet have been standing within your gates, O Jerusalem!" (Ps. 122:1–2).

Does this psalm bring the hope of the beginning and the joy felt upon arrival too close together? No. It brings out the mystery of the Church: in the Church, "have been" and "have yet to come" are two inseparable aspects. "*Advent*," of course, emphasizes anticipation. We are hoping for Jesus the Savior, who was incarnated, died for us, and rose for us two thousand years ago. With that "have been" there is the "have yet to come"—for Christ has accomplished salvation for us, and we look forward with confidence to His glorious coming, to the successful fulfillment of our salvation.

Meditation 3

The great things the Lord has prepared for us

Many people would agree that being "active" is better than being "passive," as being "active" is more proactive. When we assess a person's personality, being active is regarded as merit, and being creative in such "activeness" is even more appreciated. Yet many things in life require you not to do but "to tolerate." You have to tolerate it when someone does not care about you and when someone is ungrateful for the good you have done for him. You may also have to endure some moments of injustice (which, indeed, do not deserve being given too much importance). You, too, have to face this reality by tolerating your own shortcomings and limitations as well as some irreversible inborn defects. After all, you have to admit that you are not as good as others in some respects!

Nietzsche and many people of modern times despise the virtues of patience and humility, calling them "slavish." What they despise even more, and what they regard as "inert," is a person's "dependence" on others so that he does not pull himself together to "fight." Yet there are some people who have nothing to support their fight. Saying that they are lazy is not just. An example of this is discriminating against those who rely on social security or against new immigrants.

"It is more blessed to give than to receive" (Acts 20:35). This is certainly a golden rule. But some people have nothing at all. How can we expect them to give?

In relationships between people, we can see that "passivity" is sometimes unavoidable and is not necessarily dishonorable. In the relationship between man and God, it is even our role to be "passive." Our existence, our life, was created out of nothing by God, and God freely gives us salvation. When we were still His enemies, the Father sent His Son to redeem us and accomplish salvation for us. He has done everything for us, and we cannot even help Him out a little.

Baruch says, "Your children ... went forth from you ... but God will bring them back to you." (5:5–6). What we humans can do "actively" is to stray away from God—to commit sins. To return to Him, we can only depend on His guidance.

We don't like to feel indebted to another. It wounds our pride. But in the relationship between man and God, we cannot think this way. We are doomed to owe Him an infinite favor. Children do not care about being dependent on their parents for everything, and instead, they take it for granted. What we need is this mentality of a child.

St. Paul certainly praised the believers in Philippi for their partnership for the Gospel (Phil. 1:4–6, 8–11), but he still attributed the success to God. He said: "He who began a good work in you will bring it to completion." It is God who started it and finished it.

St. John the Baptist cried, "Prepare the way of the Lord.... All flesh shall see the salvation of God" (Luke 3:4, 6). We might ask, "Isn't it we who should return home from the land of exile? Isn't it our path made straight?" It certainly is. But it all depends on God's guidance. It is He who comes to our hearts, and then we repent and return to Him. We say, "Our repentance turns God from His wrath, and He receives us again." It is God who first receives us; only then does He teach us how to repent!

St. Augustine said that our good merits are God's gifts. What we say "we offer" during the Mass is indeed what we have received earlier from the hands of God.

Does this make us self-abasing? Modern atheists would say so. They accuse us of degrading ourselves in order to exalt God. What's more, they even say that we have created God. Saying this, we experience the most thorough "alienation": putting the goodness we deserve outside ourselves and projecting the goodness onto God. We then use this created God to suppress ourselves, setting many obstacles to our own freedom.

We would find it ridiculous for a child to say that he created his parents. But when he feels a sense of self-abasement in front of his parents because of his own identity as a son, we are pretty sure it is a rare sickness. Yet the modern man, dazzled by his achievements, embraces those fallacies in regard to God the Father!

Advent allows us Christians to experience once again the joy of having this faith. God has achieved the salvation that we have been expecting.

"The Lord has done great things for us; we are glad" (Ps. 126:3).

THEMES FOR ADVENT

Meditation 4

Hope

The psalm says, "To thee, O LORD, I lift up my soul" (25:1). This short sentence alone represents the spirit of the Advent season.

The *Catechism of the Catholic Church* tells us, "Hope is the theological virtue by which we desire the kingdom of heaven and eternal life as our happiness, placing our trust in Christ's promises and relying not on our strength, but on the help of the grace of the Holy Spirit" (CCC 1817). God is the origin, motivation, and object of hope.

The prophet Jeremiah spoke of the "good days": the Lord will "fulfill the promise," and "Judah shall be saved" (33:14–16). And in the Gospel, Jesus said the moment when "the Son of Man [comes] in a cloud with power and great glory" will be the day of our "redemption," and therefore we have to "look up and raise [our] heads" (Luke 21:27–28).

The life of faith is full of "hope" and "joy" because salvation is basically achieved, and it will finally arrive at its fullness.

Commentators of novels or plays in the modern world do not usually appreciate "happy endings." They see them as old-fashioned. Yet, at the bottom of every human heart, there is hope for a happy ending. Unfortunately, this hope is somehow unrealistic. Most endings are tragic, with hope turning into something merely imagined. But God does tell us that according to His plan, there should be a happy ending for all mankind.

God is the infinite good, and He shares His goodness with us. Through creation and salvation, He launched His plan of love. How dare we think that He could fail?

The Bible tells us that suffering and death were not in the plan of God but are the result of our sins. Two thousand years ago, God the Son became man in order to share our suffering and death. By His death, He conquered suffering and death.

If we believe in the God who has revealed Himself to us, we have reason "to hope" and "to believe firmly" that all the endings lead to life and joy. (In daily conversation, "to hope" seems to refer to something that is "uncertain." When it is the theological virtue of hope, it means to believe firmly.) After the tempest, we can expect a sunny day; "the heavens will be shaken," and there will be "a new Heaven and a new earth" (Luke 21:26; Rev. 21:1)! After all, we faithful are optimistic.

For Christians, "despairing of hope" for salvation and thinking that God could not save us is indeed a sin. But what exactly is it that you doubt? Do you doubt the power of God? Or do you doubt His mercy? The mighty and merciful God has set His goal, shown the way, and made His dwelling among us. He is always with us. His plan must succeed.

Besides "despair," the sins against hope include "presumption." "Either man presumes upon his own capacities (hoping to be able to save himself without help from on high), or he presumes upon God's almighty power or his mercy (hoping to obtain his forgiveness without conversion and glory without merit)" (CCC 2092).

It might seem easy for us to commit the sin of presumption—thinking that receiving Baptism is like buying insurance once and for all. The Lord told us in the Gospel (Luke 21:34–36), however, "Take heed to yourselves lest your hearts be weighed down with dissipation and drunkenness and cares of this life.... Watch at all times, praying."

St. Paul the Apostle said, "As you learned from us how you ought to live and to please God, just as you are doing, you do so more and more … unblamable … at the coming of our Lord Jesus" (1 Thess. 4:1; 3:13).

Besides being a time of "hope and joy," Advent is a time of "vigilance and preparation."

To you, O Lord, I lift up my soul "wholeheartedly"!

Before my episcopal ordination, I asked a fellow Salesian brother to design my coat of arms and indicated some of the themes I wished to include. When he showed me the draft, I saw that there were three places in the design that went beyond the framework. I remarked that this was out of the norm. He said, "But you are just that intrusive." He actually wanted to express my character in the coat of arms. The authority of the artist is absolute, and I was not allowed to dispute.

The liturgy of Advent nourishes our *hope*. Time and again in the Eucharist we pray, "Lord, all that we have are Your gifts"; "Lord, without You, we can do nothing. Grant us the strength to do good"; "Lord, grant us Your wisdom and teach us discernment in the midst of the events of this world and to pursue the happiness of Heaven"; "Lord, we are ashamed of our sins, and we are not worthy to be Your followers. Through the redemption by Your Son, grant us forgiveness and joy in serving You."

It is clear that the virtue of hope is "out of bounds." We are fearless because we trust in God and not in ourselves. I am writing this on Tuesday of the third week of Advent. The first reading of today is from the prophet Zephaniah: "On that day ... I will remove from your midst your proudly exultant ones.... I will leave in the midst of you a people humble and lowly. They shall seek refuge in the name of the LORD" (3:11–12). In the Gospel, Jesus said to the chief priests and the elders of the people, "Tax collectors and the harlots go into the kingdom of God before you" because they listened to John the Baptist and repented. "You did not ... repent and believe him" (Matt. 21:31–32).

Christmas is approaching. May we, like the shepherds and the Wise Men from the East, like Joseph and Mary, welcome the coming of the Holy Infant. If we feel that we belong to the group of "great sinners," let us not despair. Jesus is born precisely for us. Let us not imitate the innkeepers of Bethlehem or the inhabitants of Jerusalem, the chief priests and the elders of the people, the cruel Herod. They closed their hearts to the poor, and so to Jesus. But we should pray for such as these and ask God to break open the doors of their hearts, to melt their hearts of stone, because they, too, are the children of God.

Meditation 5

Vigilance and preparation

Who likes darkness? Isn't the light sure to prevail? Unfortunately, it is not necessarily so. Darkness often tempts us. In the dark, we can do shady things. The forbidden fruit often has its appeal. People want to "know good and evil" and control their own lives (see Gen. 3:5). Can't we live happily without God bossing us around? Materialism, utilitarianism, and hedonism sell themselves in the most exquisite packaging. What the media offers us every day is nothing but "eating, drinking, and being merry" (see Luke 12:19) and nasty acts of "debauchery and licentiousness . . . quarreling and jealousy" (Rom. 13:13).

Have we believers already made our choice? Yes. But on the journey between "beginning" and "arrival," we could still get lost. So the second state of mind for Advent is "vigilance and preparation."

We are to put on the armor of light and the new self of Christ!

Someone met St. John Bosco and asked him, "Fr. Bosco, where are you going?" Fr. Bosco replied, "I'm on my way to Heaven."

Meditation 6

Repentance

The liturgical color of Advent is purple, which is also the color of Lent. Purple bears the meaning of repentance. We generally understand repentance as we suffer to make up for our sins. In fact, repentance is primarily an internal conversion. St. John the Baptist cried out: “Repent, for the kingdom of heaven is at hand.” “Then went out to him Jerusalem and all Judea and all the region about the Jordan … confessing their sins” (Matt. 3:2, 5–6). “Confessing” and “turning back” are the fundamental meanings of *repentance*. We must come around, trust God, and recognize Him as the Lord.

Does suffering have no connection with repentance then? Repentance entails suffering. When people sin, they do not offend God for no reason. To be tempted is to face a choice: whether we listen to God or pursue an illusory "good"—that is, an action or enjoyment that we think can satisfy us. When we sin, we know that the act or enjoyment, or its influence or ways, contradicts God's will. Yet we still want it and shut our hearts to God. To repent is to admit that we have made a wrong choice and to reopen our hearts to God. We welcome Him as our Lord again.

The things that we have pursued and enjoyed still have their attractiveness, however. If they have become habits, it is more difficult for us to get rid of them. This is why we have to suffer hardship. Our suffering is of no use to God; all He wants is our love. But, for us, suffering hardship is vital, for we can forge ourselves, liberate ourselves, eliminate obstacles, and follow God attentively by suffering. To ensure success, we not only give up sinful behavior but also sacrifice willingly some pleasures that are not sinful. In fact, all those who pursue ideals suffer hardship, for they want to be free to pursue their goals. "No pain, no gain," as the saying goes. Suffering is a tool by which we prepare the way of the Lord in our hearts and make it straight.

"The time is fulfilled, and the kingdom of God is at hand" (Mark 1:15). These were the opening lines of Jesus' preaching in Galilee. In fact, the kingdom of God has arrived, because it is Jesus Christ Himself. All the words of the prophets were beginning to be realized. The Messiah, who had been expected for generations, had appeared before us. The "last Adam" had come (1 Cor. 15:45), and He would later transform the fate of humanity and usher in a new dawn. God's grand plan had entered its final stage. Two thousand years later, we are celebrating the beginning of this salvation.

What St. Paul said in 1 Corinthians has a lot to do with the fact that "the kingdom of God is at hand." "The time is running out," he said. Now that Jesus Christ has come, His Second Coming is certainly only a matter of time. Since the World to Come is at hand, the consummation of salvation is, of course, a matter in progress as well.

"For the form of this world is passing away," he added (1 Cor. 7:31). In the face of our great salvation, all values in the world have become trivial: joy or sorrow, wealth or poverty, marriage or celibacy—the distinctions between these are not too important.

From this perspective, it is easier to understand how Jesus could command some people, "Come after me!" Unlike other teachers, who demand only that their disciples accept their teachings, Jesus Christ asked them to let go of everything and follow Him on a life of nomadic mission.

One theme of the Great Jubilee of 2000 was "repentance" or "conversion." To "repent" is to change direction: from self-centeredness to surrendering oneself to the will of God. The will of God is miraculous and unpredictable and can be far removed from our own will. That is why we are often faced with shocks and surprises. God constantly reaches out to us and makes requests of us. Only a profound "eschatological consciousness" can liberate our minds and open our heart to the coming of God.

Unfortunately, it is rather easy for us to view the kingdom of Heaven as some distant goal and a permanent home for the far future. Then we become insensitive to, or even resist, God's continuous calling.

The story of Jonah the prophet is a good cautionary tale. Jonah initially showed reluctance to follow God's summons to deliver His judgment on the city of Nineveh, for fear that they would repent after hearing it. In the end, he grudgingly went to Nineveh. Upon hearing his warning, the Ninevites did repent and abandon their wickedness. God forgave and spared them. Jonah was displeased, and he disapproved of God's mercy. As it turned out, it was he who needed to repent rather than the people of Nineveh.

I am afraid we are too accustomed to think that priests should preach the importance of repentance to the believers, and believers should do the same to nonbelievers. Of course we have to focus on evangelization, and the Great Jubilee has given us one more motivation: to bring true light to those who are still in darkness. Healing broken hearts with true consolation must be an imperative in the year of mercy.[1] When preaching the gospel to others, however, we must first reflect on ourselves: Am I letting the gospel guide my thoughts and my will? Or am I unknowingly letting secularity become assimilated into my mind? Is my faith bearing the fruit of charity, or has it become so disconnected from real life that it is but an hourly adornment that repeats every week?

On the contrary, look at the so-called "heathens" around us. Many of them are righteous people who are self-disciplined and act according to their consciences. They do not complain in adversity, but in happiness they are willing to give alms, do good deeds, and practice virtues. Some even sacrifice their personal interests to serve society and benefit mankind. All they are missing is the title "Christian."

Preaching the importance of repentance is the prerogative of us clergymen, but the example of the prophet Jonah reminds us to reflect constantly on ourselves: "Do I need to repent myself?" Is priesthood a mission or a mere profession

[1] This text was written during the Jubilee Year 2000. —Ed.

for me? Do I remember that the Lord said, "Whoever would be first among you must be your slave" (Matt. 20:27)?

Look around us. Many lay brothers and sisters give more for their faith—far more—than we clergy ever have! And yet they have so much respect and love for us clergymen. As a matter of fact, I'm afraid we are not even worthy to "untie their sandal straps" (see Luke 3:16).

"Repent and believe in the Gospel!"

Meditation 7

Rejoice!

The Entrance Antiphon, "Rejoice in the Lord always," taken from Philippians 4:4, has brought us the theme of this Sunday:[2] "Again I will say, Rejoice!" The Lord is near.

The Lord is near. (Indeed, He is here!) It is the reason for joy. The merciful and mighty God has been with us for the past two thousand years. We "have no anxiety about anything, but in everything by prayer and supplication with thanksgiving let your requests be made known to God" (Phil. 4:6).

The prophet Zephaniah called on the daughter of Zion to shout for joy, to be glad and to exult. He explained the reason for this joy: "The LORD has removed the judgment

[2] Third Sunday of Advent.

against you, he has turned away your enemies. . . . The LORD, your God is . . . a mighty savior" (see 3:15, 17, NABRE).

Isaiah praised the Lord, for He is "the Holy One of Israel . . . our strength and our salvation" (see Isa. 12:2, 6).

In the Gospel (Luke 3:10–18), St. John the Baptist said, "He who is mightier than I is coming."

The joy of Advent comes solely from the merciful God. He has removed the judgment against us sinners. His judgment is always just. Truly, we are sinners. We can never challenge the judgment, and only God can remove it. He has written off our debt once and for all, a debt we could never pay off.

Our enemy is strong and powerful. Apart from the Original Sin passed on from our first parents, we have added the sins we have committed ourselves. This evil force is constantly devouring the weak among mankind.

The might of God is greater than the sin of man. God has turned away our enemies. Humanity's failure began with the fruit of a tree—the tree of the knowledge of good and evil in the Garden of Eden—but Jesus redeemed us on a tree—the holy wood of the Cross.

The crowd asked John the Baptist, "What shall we do?" (Luke 3:12). When God touches our hearts and we repent, we surely will ask the same question. John's answer points to things that we should practice especially during Advent: spiritual poverty and charity. We do not let our materialistic desires occupy our hearts. This not only prohibits us from accumulating wealth by using unethical means but requires us to be content—without greed. We not only must restrain from thinking of ill-gotten gains but should be willing to share with others what we legitimately own.

The functions of spiritual poverty and charity are nothing more than cleansing our hearts and preventing selfishness from hardening them. When Jesus can come into our hearts, He will accomplish everything.

The prophet Zephaniah (see 3:14–18) asked the Israelites to be glad and said, "The LORD your God will rejoice over you with gladness.... He will sing joyfully because of you" God will rejoice "because of me." What a wonderful thing that is! God is the infinite good. There is nothing He lacks, and we have nothing to offer Him in return. How could we make Him joyful?

"It is more blessed to give than to receive" (Acts 20:35). God is the source of this infinite good. His joy could only be giving, giving continuously, and "renewing us in His love" constantly. Our being able to make Him rejoice is His given grace. How can we not allow Him to love us?

ST. JOHN THE BAPTIST AND ST. JOSEPH

Meditation 8

St. John the Baptist

When preaching the doctrine of repentance, St. John the Baptist set himself as an example and lived a hard life. "What are you going to see? A man in fancy clothes?" No, he "wore a garment of camel's hair, and a leather girdle around his waist; and his food was locusts and wild honey" (see Matt. 11:8; 3:4).

John's preaching was persuasive because of his example of hardship. Those saints who effectively reformed the Church in history were similar. St. Francis of Assisi was transformed from a rich boy into a beggar, and thus he awakened the conscience of the leaders of his time who were indulging in luxury.

St. John the Baptist is an important figure in Advent. At the very beginning of his Gospel, Mark introduces us to the "messenger" of the Savior, whose task is to exclaim, "Prepare the way of the Lord!" (1:3).

In the book of Isaiah (40:1–5; 9–11), a voice cries out, "In the wilderness prepare the way of the LORD"; such was the way the Israelites returned from their exile to their ancestral home. In the Gospel of Mark, there is also a voice in the wilderness: "Prepare the way of the Lord"; such is the way of opening our hearts for Jesus Christ.

Today, this "way" has a richer meaning to us, of course. Jesus has come, and He said, "I am the way" (John 14:6). It is a two-way path through which God comes to us and we see and touch His love; and through Jesus Christ, we can return to the embrace of our heavenly Father. Jesus Christ is the way to "come" and thus also the way to "return." He is God the Son made flesh; as such, He can reach out to us: "Come, follow me!"

The Church has inherited John's mission to introduce this "way" to everyone. The Church must speak loudly of Jesus Christ, who was born in Bethlehem, grew up in Nazareth, preached in Palestine, died outside the city of Jerusalem, and rose again on the third day. As Paul said, "Woe to me if I do not preach the gospel!" (1 Cor. 9:16).

By emptying Himself into a path, Jesus leads us through, introduces us to God's love, and convinces us to follow Him on the way of faith. Faith is the only way to God. Abraham left his home to embark on a journey of unknown destination but with complete faith in God. For forty years, the Israelites traveled a long, tortuous road in the wilderness. Jesus took the Way of the Cross but also the Way of the Passover: through death He reached eternal life.

Advent demands that we recall how God has come to us and reflect on whether we are treading the way back to God.

The Church celebrates the Nativity of St. John the Baptist with the rank of a solemnity. St. John has a higher status among the saints, possibly because Jesus said, "I tell you, among those born of women, none is greater than John" (Luke 7:28).

The beginning of the Gospel of Luke describes the births of John and Jesus almost symmetrically: the announcement of the angels, the canticles praising God, and the joyful reaction of the people. It is worth mentioning that besides the nativities of Jesus and Our Lady and John the Baptist, the Church does not celebrate the birthdays of saints. It is worth more to celebrate the day of the death of the saints (the day of their entrance into Heaven) because we are all sinners at birth, but John had already received the blessing of the Savior when he was in the womb of his mother.

Acts 13:16–26 records St. Paul the Apostle's first address in the synagogue. In his speech, Paul mentions John, who plays an essential role in the history of salvation. Among the members of the early Church, there were possibly many disciples of John, who made a humble statement about his identity and encouraged his disciples to follow Jesus.

"The Servant's Mission" (Isa. 49:1–6) initially referred to the Messiah, the real Israel. Today, the Church uses the same poem to describe John the Baptist, although the text lists the characteristics of all prophets.

John possesses the two characteristics of a true prophet. First, the Lord calls prophets to speak in the name of God ("my mouth like a sword," "an arrow," "a light to the nations"). Second, the Lord protects them ("in the shadow of his hand he hid me," "in his quiver he hid me")—though this protection does not exclude difficulties and failures ("I have labored in vain, I have spent my strength for nothing").

John's preaching on conversion seemed to be very successful. However, from man's perspective, his ending was a failure.

He was imprisoned for admonishing Herod for his indecencies. Failing to reject the request of a girl, Herod even ordered John to be killed. John was a great prophet. Inspired by the Holy Spirit, his father, Zechariah, said, "And you, child, will be called prophet of the Most High" (Luke 1:76). Jesus also said, "What did you go out into the wilderness to behold?... A prophet? Yes, I tell you, and more than a prophet" (Matt. 11:7, 9). Before revealing His divinity, Jesus was willing to be known as a prophet. The most important characteristic of a prophet is to speak the words of God. Jesus is the "Word" of the Father. When He was incarnated and became man, He told us all the secrets He heard from His Father.

The dogmatic constitution *Lumen Gentium*, which was written by the Fathers of the Second Vatican Council, stresses that the faithful, by Baptism, are made sharers in the priestly, prophetical, and kingly functions of Christ. As mentioned here, a prophet has the dignity of conversing with God and passing on the word of God to others.

On May 27, 2001, Pope John Paul II said in his message for World Communications Day, "In the secret of our heart, we have listened to the truth of Jesus; now we must proclaim that truth from the housetops" (no. 1). We have to help the people of modern times to answer questions about their lives: "Who am I? Where have I come from, and where am I going?" Jesus "fully reveals man to himself and brings to light his high calling," and "the Gospel offers the pearl of great price for which all are searching" (no. 2). Those who refute the truth would think otherwise, but the pope said, "Just as the early witnesses to the Good News did not retreat when faced with opposition, neither should Christ's followers do so today" (no. 3).

As our parishes encouraged forming social-concern groups, the diocese stressed that there should be a balance between the roles of "servant" and "prophet." Some people have asked why the Church doesn't draw attention to the priestly and kingly roles of the laypeople at the same time. In fact, a prophet's role in "social concern" is to highlight his specific perspective. The role of a servant is stressed in his service, while the role of a prophet is to criticize society and its systems according to the standard of the Gospel. It is more like the mission of the prophet Jeremiah, "to pluck up and to break down, to destroy and to overthrow, to build and to plant" (1:10). That was what John the Baptist did—telling Herod, "It is not lawful" (Matt. 14:4).

Pope John Paul II also said that "Christians ... have a prophetic task ... to speak out against the false gods and idols of the day—materialism, hedonism, consumerism, narrow nationalism." Let us "preach the truth of Jesus ever more boldly and joyfully from the housetops, so that all men and women may hear about the love" of God (no. 4). Amen.

John the Baptist said, "Even now the axe is laid to the root of the trees" (Matt. 3:10). "His winnowing fork is in his hand, and he will clear his threshing floor.... The chaff he will burn with unquenchable fire" (Matt. 3:12). God has given us many opportunities, waiting for our repentance. We cannot test Him indefinitely. Perhaps this Advent is the last chance He will give us. If we miss it, then let us not say that God judges and punishes us; it is we who exclude ourselves from God's love when we sin.

Meditation 9

The drama of St. Joseph

Joseph was enlightened by an angel, as we read in Matthew 1:18–24. These verses in the Gospel indicate that Jesus was the "Emmanuel" prophesied by Isaiah. And Mary was the virgin who conceived and gave birth to Jesus. There are many such prophecies of the birth of great men in the Bible. They have a specific format: an angel appeared, gave the enlightened one a special title (son of David), answered a question (whether to marry Mary), provided proof (virgin gave birth), and determined the name of the one who would be born (Jesus the Savior).

What was Joseph's question about? It is a question that is difficult to understand and often misunderstood. Authoritative biblical scholars believe that the reason Joseph wanted to leave his fiancée, Mary, secretly could not be that he had any doubts about her; rather, he did not know whether he should be a part of this marvelous work. Obviously, the new situation was clearly not part of of his plan. What exactly was the Lord's plan that caused this new situation for him? God's angel told him that God needed his help. God's marvelous plan could not be easily understood by man at that time. He needed Joseph to marry Mary to give her protection from misunderstanding. Through Joseph, the baby could have the name of the descendant of David, and Joseph should also name the baby Jesus. Joseph was a righteous man, and once he understood God's will, he accepted it.

In Matthew 1:18–24, Joseph seems to be the protagonist, but his righteousness further highlights Mary's obedience to God's will. In this mystery of the Incarnation of the Word, Jesus is the protagonist; Mary is the first supporting character, and Joseph is the second. The name of the drama is "Obedience of Faith."

JESUS THE LORD

Meditation 10

Jesus and the prophecies

In Matthew 11:2–11, the disciples of John the Baptist asked Jesus who He is. Jesus replied, "Go and tell John what you hear and see: the blind receive their sight and the lame walk, lepers are cleansed and the deaf hear, and the dead are raised up, and the poor have good news preached to them." For Jews familiar with the Old Testament, it was obvious that Jesus asked them to compare the prophecies of Isaiah the prophet with what He had done.

The arrangement of the Advent Mass readings is quite special. The customary liturgical reading is based on the Gospel with an Old Testament text to match it; but, in Advent, almost all the readings are based on the book of Isaiah with the Gospel chapters to match it—indicating that the prophet's prophecies were fulfilled in Jesus. This contrast between the Old Testament and the words and deeds of Jesus was a powerful argument in the early Church's preaching, and it is also key to our understanding of the history of salvation.

Today, however, two thousand years after the birth of Christ, we must have more evidence to prove that the words of the prophets were fulfilled in Jesus. Christ's coming was certainly not just for the blind, the lame, the lepers, the deaf, the dead who were raised and who lived a few more years, or the poor with whom He came into contact in the Gospel. He came to save all people—everyone. If someone asks us today who Jesus is, we should have a richer answer for them. In us, and throughout the history of the Church, Christ has kept fulfilling the prophecies of the prophet.

Meditation 11

Jesus, the Lamb of God

In the Gospel, the Church, through John the Baptist's mouth, "shows" us again who Jesus is (John 1:29–34). He is the Lamb of God who takes away the sins of the world. John the Baptist, who has played an important role on the liturgical stage since the beginning of Advent, now leaves the stage with this crucial line: "Behold, the Lamb of God, who takes away the sins of the world."

Of course, this line was written by John the Evangelist. In his mind, what does "the Lamb" stand for? We can find it in the book of Revelation, which he wrote. John saw in the vision that the "Lamb" was "worthy to take the scroll and to open its seals, for thou wast slain and by thy blood didst ransom men for God from every tribe and tongue and people and nation"(5:9). In the Gospel, John deliberately points out that after Jesus died, "not a bone of him shall be broken." And this fulfills Scripture's stipulation about the Passover lamb, "You shall not break a bone of it" (John 19:36; Exod. 12:46).

This lamb is a scapegoat. It is apparent in the fourth "song of the Servant of the Lord" in the book of Isaiah. (In Aramaic, the words "*servant*" and "*lamb*" share the same root.) "But he was wounded for our transgressions, he was bruised for our iniquities. . . ." "The LORD has laid on him the iniquity of us all" (Isa. 53:5–6). As St. Paul says in 2 Corinthians 5:21: "For our sake he made him to be sin who knew no sin, so that in him we might become the righteousness of God." "He poured out his soul to death, and was numbered with the transgressors; yet he bore the sin of many, and made intercession for the transgressors" (Isa. 53:12).

In Isaiah 49 is the second song of "the Servant of the Lord." As John did in the book of Revelation, this hymn emphasizes the victory and glory of the "Servant of the Lord"—the "Lamb." His sacrifice absolved the sin of "the world." He was "a light to the nations," and His "salvation may reach to the end of the earth" (Isa. 49:6).

John said, "I have seen and testified." Testifying is also the mission of the Church. Faithful generations after generations, especially the martyrs and the missionaries, testified to this "Lamb who takes away the sin of the world."

The priest holds up the consecrated bread and says, "Behold the Lamb of God, behold Him who takes away the sins of the world!" Do we experience the presence of the Son of God as John did? When the priest says, "The Body of Christ," does our response, "Amen," come from the bottom of our hearts?

Lord, I believe You have saved me and everyone in the world. You have now brought the grace of salvation into my heart again. Please allow me to experience Your presence, and help me to bear witness to You in my life.

Meditation 12

The Second Coming

By nature, humans seek stability or even hope that matters can be put right once and for all, but where is the cornerstone for stability? What do humans rely upon?

The Israelites are the Chosen People of God. God made them to be His people, and He vowed to be their God, their support. However, throughout history, Israel has time and time again betrayed their faith in God and misplaced their trust in covenants with other nations. The results? Defeat, subjugation, and exile.

In the era of Jesus Christ, their leaders had perverted the true meaning of the Mosaic Covenant, straining the relationship between God and man. Being the descendants of Abraham seemed like a free pass for everything. The Temple became a symbol of all their special graces. All must journey there to become subjects of Israel. Nevertheless, the fall of Jerusalem and the destruction of the Temple around AD 70 exposed the flaws in that belief.

People of today are keen on depending solely on themselves, thinking that technological advancements will be the solution to everything and that with progress in psychology and sociology, all problems of humanity and society will be untangled. This could not be any further from the truth. Science has brought us powerful, all-life-destroying weapons; meanwhile, poverty and disease have not ceased to exist. Instead, they continue to ravage with their many new forms. Disputes and wars between groups and races occur daily. Abortions, divorces, suicides, and mental illnesses are on the rise, and it seems particularly worse in countries with exceptional social welfare systems.

It is impossible to deny the ruinous situation with a clear conscience. In his prayer, Isaiah described this exact scenario: "We sinned; in our sins we have been a long time. We have all become like one who is unclean, and all our righteous deeds are like a polluted garment. We all fade like a leaf, and our iniquities, like the wind, take us away" (64:5–6). And the root cause? "O LORD, why dost thou make us err from thy ways and harden our heart, so that we fear thee not?" (Isa. 63:17). If we stray away from God and turn to rely on ourselves, this will be the tragic end that awaits us.

Being aware of one's errors is an important first step on the path of repentance. Turn back and surrender to God, and the situation can flip around. On the First Sunday of Advent,[3] the Church wakes us from our false sense of self-reliance. Through the words of Isaiah, we pray, "Oh, that you would tear open the heavens and come down, with the mountains quaking before you!" (see Is. 64:1). In Psalm 80, the responsorial verse goes, "Restore us, O God; let thy face shine, that we may be saved" (v. 3).

We call God our "Father" and "Savior" (Isa. 63:16–17, 19; 64:2–7). The relationship between us and God is like "a young vine" and "the gardener who planted it with his own hands" (see Ps. 80:8) or like "the clay" and "the potter" (Isa. 64:8). We hold our faith in God with utmost confidence because He began His good work in us long ago. As Paul the Apostle said to the Corinthians:

> I give thanks to God always for you because of the grace of God which was given you in Christ Jesus, that in every way you were enriched in him with all

[3] Year B.

> speech and all knowledge—even as the testimony to Christ was confirmed among you—so that you are not lacking in any spiritual gift, as you wait for the revealing of our Lord Jesus Christ; who will sustain you to the end, guiltless in the day of our Lord Jesus Christ. (1 Cor. 1:4–8)

This is the message of Advent: Jesus Christ has come, but He will come again, and we must prepare for His Second Coming. We were incapable of working with Him when He began His good work (and we even turned our backs to Him because of our sins), but to bring His work to fruition, our cooperation is indispensable.

The Gospel (Mark 13:33–37) emphasizes that we must, at all times, have a humble, prudent, and cooperative attitude toward our salvation: "Be watchful! Be alert!" There is no one-and-done in this world because the grace of God never ceases to flow toward us, and we must always be ready to welcome Him.

Of course, being "humble and prudent" does not mean we should be frightened—because the salvation that we already received has definitively shown us the perfect end that has yet to come. In fact, Advent also represents our entire life in faith: we should rejoice and give thanks for the salvation we have received and work tirelessly for the future with all our might.

Advent commemorates the salvation that has already been and the salvation that has yet to come. The book of Isaiah emphasizes the "have dones" three times ("that her time of service has ended, that her iniquity is pardoned, that she has received from the LORD's hand double for all her sins") and cries out resoundingly, "Behold your God!" (40:1–5, 9). Yet the Second Letter of Peter (3:8–14) emphasizes that the day of God has yet to come, and we must be "waiting for and hastening the coming of the day of God."

Despite the confusion, there is not actually any contradiction between the "has been" and the "has yet to come." Isaiah's prophecies were indeed primarily related to that specific era, but they also foretold the coming of Jesus Christ and the beginning of the apocalypse. But His salvation will lead us to the perfect end.

The Second Letter of Peter was written at the end of the Apostolic Age. Some followers thought the Resurrection of Jesus Christ would be very close to His Second Coming. They waited and waited, but there was no sign of His Second Coming. Peter then reminded them that the close link between these two events should not be measured in years but that Jesus Christ would surely return in glory at some time, and it was important that they prepare "diligently" while they waited.

When we talk about the "last days," we tend to ask many questions. Unfortunately, many of them are unanswerable. We are such strange creatures that we always want to seek what we should not know or what we do not need to know. "When will the end of the world come?" "How many people will be saved?" "What is Heaven really like?" "Why did God create Hell?" "Why doesn't God let us know the number of years in our lives so that we can make plans?"

We want to know because we want to plan, we want to have control over our lives, and we want to arrange everything ourselves. The truth is, the life of each of us is not something we plan out but is a gift from God, a calling from God. And we must respond to that calling, since the calling is out of love.

There are many things in life that we need to plan and arrange, but before God, the basic attitudes of life should be *acceptance*, *patience*, *trust*, *hope*, *devotion*, and even *adventure*.

The Creator also accepts risks. He proposes His plan of love but does not force us to carry it out. He gives us autonomy and asks us to trust Him but is willing to risk our rejection.

Ultimately, what are the so-called "risks" we are taking? On God's side, everything has been done and given to us; everything is guaranteed!

The plan of love of God has reached its final stage: Jesus Christ has accomplished salvation. "For by a single offering he has perfected for all time those who are sanctified" (Heb. 10:14). He "has taken His seat "at the right hand of God" until the day on which "the Son of Man [will come] in clouds with great power and glory, and then He will … gather His elect from the four winds, from the ends of the earth to the ends of heaven" (Heb. 10:12; Mark 13:26–27). At that time, "everyone whose name shall be found written in the book" "shall be delivered" (Dan. 12:1).

Will there be people not "found written in the book"? It is quite possible, but only those who exclude themselves from love exclude themselves from the book of life. Death does not come from God. To depart from God is to choose death. Life and death are options placed in front of us, and it is up to us to make our own choice.

Now that our goal is clear and the right choice has been made, the road ahead is still treacherous and full of unknowns. Of course, when we make promises, they are about the future, but we do not yet know what the future will look like. The value of a promise lies in the basis of "no matter what the future holds."

When a man and a woman get married, they promise each other that they will always love each other, for better, for worse, for richer, for poorer, in sickness and health, until death do them part.

St. John Bosco said that we cannot go to Heaven in a carriage. In a dream, he saw himself and his brothers from the Salesian Society walking in a rose garden, with thorns surrounding the paths they took!

There will be "a great tribulation" before the revelation of the glory of God (Dan. 12:1–3; Mark 13:24–32). The *Catechism of the Catholic Church* particularly affirms this point. I was deeply moved when I first read it. Hereby I transcribe the two specific verses:

> Before Christ's second coming the Church must pass through a final trial that will shake the faith of many believers (cf. Luke 18:8; Matt. 24:12). The persecution that accompanies her pilgrimage on earth (cf. Luke 21:12; John 15:19–20) will unveil the "mystery of iniquity" in the form of a religious deception offering men an apparent solution to their problems at

> the price of apostasy from the truth. The supreme religious deception is that of the Antichrist, a pseudo-messianism by which man glorifies himself in place of God and of his Messiah come in the flesh (cf. 2 Thess. 2:4–12; 1 Thess. 5:2–3; 2 John 7; 1 John 2:18, 22). (675)

> The kingdom will be fulfilled, then, not by a historic triumph of the Church through a progressive ascendancy, but only by God's victory over the final unleashing of evil. (677)

Let us not be afraid! In this calamity, we are protected by the archangel Michael (see Daniel 12:1–3), and all the saints in the past, especially the martyrs. Also, we are led by the living representative of Jesus Christ. Let us join hands and march forward with courage!

Part II

CHRISTMAS

A CHILD IS BORN FOR US

Meditation 13

Christ the Savior is born

Christ is born. Let the world rejoice! During Advent, the Church's liturgy makes use of the Gospel readings to show that the prophecy of Isaiah is fulfilled in Jesus: He makes the blind see, the deaf hear, and the lame walk and consoles broken hearts. But the greatest miracle is to have sins forgiven. "My child, your sins are forgiven" (Mark 2:5). That is the true liberation!

However, it is strange that this sentence is not always welcome. The Pharisees questioned Jesus: "Where did He get the authority to forgive sins?" People of our generation would even ask, "You forgive my sins? Am I a sinner?"

Some people think that since they have not killed anyone, they are not sinners! Some think that the Ten Commandments are only an ideal; they aim too high. We do not have to take them seriously. Some admit that their moral lives are not up to standard, but they easily exonerate themselves: there are too many temptations; there is too much pressure. Some do not even recognize what sin is. Some think that it is morbid to have a sense of guilt because sin does not exist.

For these people, the coming of Christmas means holidays, gatherings, parties, gifts, and so forth. They waste a precious opportunity. Let us search the depth of our hearts and acknowledge that we are sinners, that we have denied the grace of God, that our behaviors have gone far away from God, that we are sick and need the Divine Healer from Heaven to heal us.

Let us judge ourselves. If we do so, the Judge will pronounce our innocence! This is indeed a very profitable deal.

Repentance demands a change. "Yours sins are forgiven. Do not sin again." Only a change in our behavior can show that our repentance is true. In fact, we cannot deceive God or ourselves. Our consciences will tell us whether we are truly repentant.

There are times when we have to show our bothers and sisters that we are truly repentant. If a sin is publicly known or is against the laws of the Church, the repentance will have to be public. If not, the bad example given cannot be amended. If those who have a ministry in the Church committed an offense against the laws of the Church, the responsibility to make public amends is greater.

The Church is a Mother. She forgives easily. But in forgiving, it is necessary to give penance. If the Church misleads the faithful into thinking that an offense against the laws of the Church is a triviality, she is responsible for those who might easily commit such offenses in the future.

St. John the Baptist has led us to Christmas. He has the spirit of Isaiah in having no tolerance regarding sins. He said no to Herod. May the precursor of Jesus help us to be "steadfast." To be "steadfast in truth" is our glory as Christians. Be a person of character!

Do you feel that what has been written above is not compatible with the spirit of gentleness of Christmas? Let us not forget this: while we kneel before the stable, we shall soon witness the blood of St. Stephen.[4] Martyrdom is the logical, inevitable conclusion of the Christmas story!

[4] The feast of St. Stephen, the first Christian martyr, is on December 26. —Ed.

Meditation 14

A Child is born

According to theological understanding, the *now*-existing Jesus Christ has risen from the dead and is in glory in Heaven. But, on Christmas, let us recall that Jesus was born a baby in Bethlehem and was placed in a manger. It was St. Francis who started the tradition of the Nativity scene. When entering the religious order, St. Thérèse of Lisieux took "of the Child Jesus" as part of her new name. So let us also come before the manger with the mentality of a child. Jesus in the manger is the Word become flesh and blood. Previously, humans could not see and touch the Lord, or they would die. Now it is possible. He dwells among us and has become one among us.

St. Paul said, "the grace of God has appeared for the salvation of all men" and added that He saved us "when the goodness and loving kindness of God our Savior appeared" (Titus 2:11; 3:4).

Kindness and generous love are especially shown in His forbearance. When He was born, there was no inn in Bethlehem that could accommodate Him. He tolerated not only the people of Bethlehem of the time but all human beings who lived through every age, everywhere in the world. That includes me; that includes you. St. John said, "He came to his own home, and his own people received him not," adding, "The light shines in the darkness.... The true light that enlightens every man was coming into the world ... yet the world knew him not" (John 1:5, 9–10).

Because of His excessive love for us, God sent us His Son in the likeness of our sinful bodies (cf. Rom. 8:3)—a fragile infant laid in a manger; only with the help of an angel He could escape the attempt on His life. He wanted to experience all the hardships of human existence, hoping that we might finally trust Him and recognize Him as one of us.

God decided from eternity to create man and desired to make covenant with Him. Through the prophets, He said repeatedly that He wants to be our God and wants us to be His people.

What has He to gain from this? He is infinite goodness; man is nothingness. Whatever goodness is in man is His gift. God doesn't love man because man is lovable: man is lovable only because God has loved him first. Man still had hesitations and did not trust God (the Original Sin is the paradigm of all sins), so God further shortened the distance and decided to come into our midst as our Brother, Friend, and Companion in the journey. His name is Emmanuel (God with us) (Matt. 1:23). Even at the end of His earthly journey, He didn't want to leave us, and before His Passover to Heaven, He invented a marvelous way to remain with us: hiding Himself in the sacrament of the Eucharist, setting up His tent on earth. If Moses could say, "What great nation is there that has a god so near to it as the LORD our God is to us?," how much more truly we should appreciate that God really lives in our midst!

This Christmas, let us finally surrender to the "excessive" love of God, never again to force Him to complain, as He did when appearing to St. Margaret: "How much this heart loves man but receives only indifference in return."

Let us approach Him and revere Him in the Eucharist, receive Him often into our hearts, keep Him company, and adore Him.

As God took on human nature, mankind and each man shared His divinity; Jesus became present in each person, especially in the least of our brothers. Let us see Him in each weak person, revere Him, and care for Him, as did the Good Samaritan.

This Jesus "present in our midst" must be the example especially for pastors, parents, and leaders in society.

Pastors are bound to consecrate themselves selflessly to their flock. Their time and energy no more belong to them; especially when the wolf comes, the pastor must be ready to sacrifice his life to defend his flock.

The presence of their parents is essential for the healthy growth of children. The company of their mothers and fathers is much more precious than any gift their parents can offer. Dear fathers and mothers, are you aware that your little Jesus is waiting for you, the way a flower expects the sunshine and water?

Leaders in society must be the servants of the people. To be close to the people should be not a mere tactic but a sincere basic attitude. In order to think and feel in consonance with the people, leaders must be in constant contact with the grassroots people and have respect for them. All their policies must be based on the people's well-being.

Many problems have surfaced recently in our society. Isn't it because we abandoned the above-mentioned criterion of good governance? The economic factor—nay, the shortsighted economic gain—has become the only guide in policymaking; distribution of wealth was taken as in apposition to creation of wealth, the gap between the rich and the poor dangerously widened. In men, it is a shame; in civilizations, it is decadence!

The angel sang in the sky of Bethlehem: "Glory to God in the highest, and on earth peace among men with whom he is pleased" (Luke 2:14). We must not despair; God's love is unfailing. It is up to us to welcome Him; the conversion consists in making just one step. May the peace of God come to our hearts and accompany us throughout all the days of this year.

Meditation 15

The true center of human reunion is the incarnated Son of God

Seeing the surrounding valley slumbering in darkness or the morning sun illuminating the walls of the Holy City, every Israelite would be proud. The prophet Isaiah probably imagined such a vision as he prophesied about the glorious day of the Lord: Jerusalem would be the center of the world, and all nations would come to her. The Israelites, especially in the throes of history, looked forward to this glorious day.

In fact, God's plan goes far beyond this image. The true center of human reunion is not Jerusalem but the incarnated

Son of God. He united the entire human race in Himself; all men, regardless of race or gender, whether saints or sinners, could be "partakers of the promise in Christ Jesus through the gospel" (Eph. 3:6).

The Israelites' "self-centeredness" is not easy to dispel. God gave Paul a mission: to reveal the mysteries of the last days—"Gentiles [and Jews] are fellow heirs, members of the same body" (Eph. 3:6).

When the Magi from the East came to worship the new king, the mysteries started to be revealed.

Meditation 16

The big family of the Church

Faced with the challenges of modern society and the ideals stated by St. Paul, individual families might feel helpless. The foundation of our hope certainly comes from trust in the Lord, however, and thanks be to God, as He also gives us the support of the Church's big family. In the big family of the Church, we have more opportunities to listen to the words of wisdom, sing songs with gratitude, enjoy the friendship of brothers and sisters, and learn to give and serve each other.

Ours is a God-fearing home, full of life and blessings!

Meditation 17

The real sun is Jesus

Light is especially suitable to symbolize the coming of Jesus. December 25 was not necessarily the day when Jesus was born. The early Church borrowed from pagans the date they worshipped the sun god. We all know that the earth revolves around the sun in an elliptical orbit. When the earth travels to the farthest end from the sun, people feel that the power of the sun becomes weaker. But people feel the sun become warm again when the earth moves closer to it. So people began to worship the sun god, who can be "reborn" every year.

We know that the real sun is Jesus. He is the light of humanity. Darkness can never overcome Him, whose warmth sustains our lives. St. John said that "to those who received him, who believed in his name, he gave power to become children of God" (John 1:12).

A TIME FOR JOY

Meditation 18

Christmas brings joy

The angels sang, "Glory to God in the highest, and on earth peace among men with whom he is pleased" (Luke 2:14). Light, warmth, and peace are God's gifts to all humanity this Christmas. All this is also called grace and salvation. It is grace because we have won it not through our righteousness but through God's mercy; it is salvation because, as unclean sinners and sinful slaves, we should have become "forsaken," "desolate," but now Jesus' coming has turned us to be "holy people," "the redeemed of the LORD," "sought out," "a city not forsaken" (Isa. 62:4, 12). Christmas brings joy, and we share this joy like those who harvest crops or share victories.

With this new identity and in this new situation, we are called to have a new life to match it. St. Paul said that we should "renounce irreligion and worldly passions, and to live sober, upright, and godly lives in this world, awaiting our blessed hope, the appearing of the glory of our great God and Savior Jesus Christ" (Titus 2:12–13). Could it be that the Son of God came down from Heaven to accompany us on the way to Heaven and to lead us to share the eternal blessings that He has won for us?

Our joy comes from knowing who Christ is and realizing His saving power. The miracles of Christ's salvation continue to be fulfilled until the day of His glorious return, and that is what we should hope for.

If we still look sad all the time, it's probably because we've forgotten the real reason for joy or we've set our expectations on something else. Gandhi said, "You Christians are so unlike your Christ." He said that looking at the sad faces of Christians: "You could hardly be disciples of a Person who triumphed over death." Of course, human beings have natural reactions of happiness, anger, sorrow, and joy, but faith should help us not to be too excited when things succeed and not to be discouraged and disappointed when we fail. We should be glad that Christ has accomplished salvation for us; no one can take it away.

Let us listen to the words of Isaiah the prophet again, "Rejoice with joy and singing.... Be strong, fear not! Behold, your God.... He will come and save you" (35:2, 4).

Meditation 19

Rejoicing in the Lord

There were some simple, candid views in the Old Testament: God blesses the good man, so the good man is always well and succeeds in his every doing. Psalm 1 says, "Blessed is the man who walks not in the counsel of the wicked … but his delight is in the law of the LORD. … In all that he does, he prospers" (vv. 1, 3). Psalm 37 also clearly states the fates of the good and the wicked: the world is just—good is rewarded with good, and evil with evil. In the worldview of the people of the Old Testament, the rewards of good deeds were immediate in the present life.

But reality rarely conforms to this simple rule. The book of Job shattered this naive belief. Isaiah described the Messiah's duty was to "bring good tidings to the afflicted …

to bind up the brokenhearted, to proclaim liberty to the captives, and the opening of the prison to those who are bound" (Isa. 61:1). This description indirectly affirms the complex side of life. It can be said that it preaches the lesson of the Beatitudes in advance: the afflicted, the brokenhearted, the captives, the prisoners, and so on are blessed, and the Lord's Anointed Bearer of glad tidings will bring them comfort and joy.

When Jesus came, He really brought good news to the poor: "the blind receive their sight and the lame walk, lepers are cleansed and the deaf hear, and the dead are raised up" (Matt. 11:5). The people cheered, "a great prophet has arisen among us!" (Luke 7:16). Some even wanted to crown Him king. But they had misunderstood Jesus. We can borrow the words of John, "among you stands one whom you do not know" (John 1:26).

Not only the ignorant crowds, but even the apostles also did not fully understand Jesus. They were anticipating a speedy success, a ready-to-serve-style glory. Jesus had to teach them painstakingly the dialectical path of the law of suffering and joy: "Blessed are those who mourn, for they shall be comforted.... Blessed are those who are persecuted for righteousness' sake, for theirs is the kingdom of heaven" (Matt. 5:4, 10).

Both before His Passion and after His Resurrection, Jesus repeatedly stressed that the Cross was "necessary" and that it was the source of joy. Of course, what was "necessary" was not the suffering of bearing the Cross itself but the love that stood the test of the Cross, the love that placed its full faith in God, and the love that made Him willing to sacrifice Himself for us.

In His farewell to the apostles, He said, "I say to you, you will weep and lament, but the world will rejoice; you will be sorrowful, but your sorrow will turn into joy" (John 16:20).

St. Paul wrote in his Second Letter to the Corinthians, "As we share abundantly in Christ's sufferings, so through Christ we share abundantly in comfort too" (1:5). He also wrote to the Colossians, "Now I rejoice in my sufferings for your sake, and in my flesh I complete what is lacking in Christ's afflictions for the sake of his body, that is, the church" (thus completing the part that Jesus Christ left for us to take part in) (1:24).

I very much hope that you will have the opportunity to get to know these "living martyrs" who had spent decades imprisoned for their Faith. We can then witness the true peace and joy that can be derived only from the Holy Spirit.

Not everyone needs to face the dilemma between faith and imprisonment or sacrificing one's life, but in our day-to-day lives, we still have many opportunities to seek our own true peace and joy: "If you keep my commandments, you will abide in my love, just as I have kept my Father's commandments and abide in his love. These things I have spoken to you, that my joy may be in you, and that your joy may be full" (John 15:10–11).

Meditation 20

True and false joy

Once again, the rich and the poor are pitted against each other. In his Gospel, Luke emphasized the relationship between poverty and salvation. The early Church discovered very soon that living in poverty was no guarantee of Heaven, and that it was not impossible for a rich man to be saved. The Gospel of Luke says, "Blessed are you poor.... But woe to you that are rich" (6:20, 24). And the Gospel of Matthew says, "Blessed are the poor in spirit" (5:3).

Being "poor" and "poor in spirit" are, in fact, closely related. Some passages in Scripture help us understand why it is not easy for the rich to go to Heaven. There is nothing bad about money itself, but it can easily bring temptation to people and hinder the practice of being "poor in spirit."

1. The prophet Amos pointed out that it is easy for the rich to rely on their wealth, "secure on the mountain of Samaria," and to forget that the Lord is the Lord of Heaven and earth (6:1). The poor have nothing to rely on, and it is easier for them to think of their heavenly Father. The hardships of this world are supposed to make us yearn for happiness in Heaven.
2. The rich man in the parable in the Gospel went to Hell not because of his wealth but because he did not care about the poor man Lazarus (Luke 16:19–31). It is easy for the rich man to forget that the poor man is his brother and that he has the responsibility to take care of him. A Chinese adage says, "Wine and meat rot behind vermilion gates while at the roadside people freeze to death." In the eye of God, this sin will be less tolerated at the Judgment: "For I was hungry and you gave me no food, I was thirsty and you gave me no drink.... As you did it not to one of the least of these, you did it not to me" (Matt. 25:42, 45).
3. The rich people live lives that are too comfortable. Another Chinese idiom says, "Well fed and warmly clad, one then attends to lust." Likewise,

> Scripture says that those who "ate, drank, and sang "idle songs ... are not grieved over the ruin of Joseph" (Amos 6:5–6).

Let us reflect a bit on this third point. We know how important the Sabbath was in the Old Testament: one of every seven days should be a day of rest so that the people can enjoy freedom. In modern society, we strive to work only five days. It is a good thing to spend an extra day cultivating spiritual values or sharing happy moments with family. Unfortunately, people are forced to work seven days a week in many places. This is certainly not the will of God.

In modern society, the proportion of people working in service industries is getting higher and higher, and the entertainment and tourism businesses are becoming more and more diversified. This can be seen as progress, but it also has negative side effects. Some people regard entertainment as their ideal of life, and work is only for making money for entertainment.

This obsession with entertainment has led to a culture that damages society: wasting time and energy, sacrificing sleep and coping sluggishly with work. Technological progress requires the careful cooperation of many people, and a failure in one procedure can bring disastrous consequences (such as the failure of a space program due to human error).

Technological progress has placed strong and powerful machines (such as vehicles) in our hands. How dangerous it can be when there is a lack of sense of responsibility!

For some people, entertainment is like a drug. They cannot extricate themselves when they become addicted. Seeking excitement in entertainment is also like taking drugs, constantly "asking for more" and bringing a never-ending pursuit. The stimulation of the senses is nothing but pornography and violence. Some places of entertainment have become the hotbeds of sin. Again, there are those who "are not grieved over the ruin of Joseph." For some people, marriage is only a form of selfish enjoyment. They see children as a burden and do not want to bring forth new life. When they have children, they see them as accidents. The lack of vocations is a very complex problem. There can be many reasons for it, but a culture of a life of amusement is surely one of them.

The value advocated in the culture of a life of amusement is to make money and have fun. In entertainment and leisure, young people escape reality and indulge in a virtual world. The ideals of being a servant of the gospel and working silently for the kingdom of Heaven no longer draw their interest.

The "life of amusement" culture also tempts those who have joined the service team. The advice of Paul the Apostle given to Timothy is still relevant for us who are dedicated to God today, "For the love of money is the root of all evils.... But as for you, man of God, shun all this; aim at righteousness, godliness, faith, love, steadfastness, gentleness. Fight the good fight of the faith" (1 Tim. 6:10–12).

This is truly a "holy war." It is more difficult to guard against the enemy of the soul than to defend against terrorists. Let us be more alert. We should not let the enemy destroy the work of God.

LITURGICAL THEMES

Meditation 21

The Holy Family

Blessed are those who dwell in thy house!" (Ps. 84:4).
Hannah named her son Samuel because she had "asked him of the LORD." When the child was weaned, his mother brought him to Shiloh, where the house of the Lord was. She gave her child to Eli, the priest of the Lord, to offer the child to the Lord because "as long as he lives, he shall be dedicated to the LORD" (1 Sam. 1:20, 28, NABRE).

Each and every life is "asked of the Lord" and "shall be dedicated to the LORD." Indeed, everyone needs to belong to something so that they can feel safe. And only when we belong to the Lord can we have the real blessing.

In his First Letter, St. John also described the relationship between God and us as that "we abide in him and he in us" (1 John 4:13). It is easier for us to understand the relationship between parents and children: they are of the same blood. Wouldn't it be bold to describe the relationship between God and us as the relationship between parent and children? St. John insisted that we not only may be called the children of God but actually *are* children of God. Only the mystery has not yet been revealed. When it is revealed, we shall be like Him (1 John 3:1–2). For the time being, we must comply with the commandments and carry out our charitable works in order to remain in this mysterious relationship.

Luke 2:41–52 is a difficult passage. On the surface, it describes a disruption of the family order: the twelve-year-old boy no longer wants to remain under the authority of His parents! But this fact is revealed: the Holy Family of Nazareth and every family should have God as their Father.

Mary looked all over for Jesus. After three days, she found Him and said to Him, "Why have you treated us so? Behold, your father and I have been looking for you anxiously." Jesus' reply was somehow uncourteous, "How is it that you sought me? Did you not know that I must be in my Father's house?"

Mary and Joseph were too used to enjoying a human relationship with Jesus day and night. Jesus, however, always made His relationship with the heavenly Father the criterion of all His actions. Mary and Joseph needed an adjustment to their consciousness.

"Did you not know?" was how Jesus rebuked the apostles for their lack of faith. "They did not understand this saying" was how Luke described the apostles' failure to understand Jesus' prediction of His going to Jerusalem and His Passion (Luke 9:43–45; 18:34). Jesus also rebuked the two disciples He met on the road to Emmaus for being foolish and slow of heart (Luke 24:25–26).

This first "going to Jerusalem" was a prelude of His last "going to Jerusalem": three days of searching, three days of waiting: the Paschal mystery was already presented.

The wisdom of Jesus' humanity was yet to grow. However, His transcendental wisdom has already shed light in the dialogues with the scribes and His "parents." We can say that He had undertaken a Transfiguration.

He said that the only thing that matters is that "I must be in my Father's house." To do the Father's will surpasses everything else. And the Father's will for us is to "keep his commandment and love one another," as mentioned in the First Letter of John (see 5:3).

Although Mary and Joseph have not reached the maturity of faith, they at least sought it sincerely. (Forms of *seek* or *look for* appear four times in this Gospel passage.) Those who seek will finally find. His parents did not understand what Jesus said, yet they accepted it, and Our Lady "kept all these things in her heart."

How much do our families need this sincerity in "seeking" and "listening"! It seems that we enjoy the right to be supported by our family, but forget that the family requires each member to contribute. Each family member is a unique mystery. No one can try to possess anyone else. Mutual respect is the fundamental prerequisite of mutual love. The condition for mutual respect lies in this: that everyone sees the presence of the Lord in everyone else.

Only when we center our families on the heavenly Father can each one become a sweet family, a school of faith, and the gate of Heaven (*porta Coeli*).

The hymn in the Liturgy of the Hours describes the joy of the Holy Family: lead a simple, virtuous life and live peacefully. Mary is full of grace, and her heart is extremely holy. She embraces the little Jesus, kisses Him, and nurtures Him. It is a great glory in the world. Joseph is a humble gentleman, a descendant of ancient saints, and the guardian of the Virgin. The Son of God depends on him. The good name of being a foster father is praised by all ages. Jesus the Savior loves His parents and sets for us an example of obedience.

Meditation 22

Epiphany

The Magi's coming from the East to worship the newborn King and Jesus' receiving baptism from John the Baptist in the river Jordan should not be only the two mysteries bringing the Christmas season to an end but should also bring us to the start of Ordinary Time in the liturgical calendar. The fundamental messages of these two mysteries should serve as our pilot lamp as we journey through Ordinary Time.

The Epiphany is the "outburst" of salvation: Christ is the only Savior, and through His Church, His salvation "diffuses" to every person. A great light has shone upon the world. We are people full of hope. We have seen Christ's salvation, and we know we have already been living in the grace of Christ. We also know that through the Spirit of Christ, we can call God the Father our heavenly Father, and we are truly brothers and sisters. It is our glorious mission to evangelize and to care about our society. We have to build a new family of humanity with love.

Jesus received the baptism from John in place of us sinners. The Father recognized Him as His beloved Son, the One anointed and sent. He is the messenger of God, who comes to bring all mankind to the path of conversion to the Father.

Certainly, this is also the *Via Crucis* (the Way of the Cross). "My beloved Son" is at the same time "the suffering servant." (He will not cry out or shout, like a lamb led to slaughter [see Isa. 42:2; 53:7].) When we are still sweetly adoring the Holy Infant laying in the manger, the blood of St. Stephen and the Holy Innocents has made apparent the crucifix next to the stable.

We must take up all the challenges ahead with the spirit of Christmas. Let us submit ourselves to God to become the children who make the Father "well pleased" and to be "the suffering servant." We have to prepare to be persecuted for witnessing the truth and to accept death for proclaiming the "gospel of life." Let us uphold justice and fight for the rights and dignity of those who protest silently for the oppression they endure.

In the dark days, let us recall the voice of St. John Paul II. In the last days of his life, he seemed to be conquered by death, but he continued to offer wisdom and courage to all mankind. He said, "Be not afraid."

Let us go back to the manger and listen to the angels singing: "On earth peace among men with whom he is pleased" (Luke 2:14). Let us once again listen to the voice coming down from the heavens: "Listen to Him, my beloved Son and the suffering servant. It is His suffering and death that have brought the mankind life and joy."

The visit of the Magi from the East, the baptism of Jesus by John, and the turning of water into wine at the wedding at Cana were three incidents in which our Lord manifested Himself to the world. In the first chapter of his Gospel, St. John writes, "The Word became flesh and dwelt among us" (v. 14). When we hear this, we may not think of this Incarnate God mingling with mankind so well and even taking His disciples to a wedding banquet.

John the Baptist has a much different style. He is out of touch with the mundane. His living aloof from the secular world tells us that when those who are distant from God struggle to find Him, they won't be in for an easy time.

Jesus was certainly not in Cana for mere fun. He was there to bring *joy*. And Mary, more often than not, forgot herself and cared for others. She became her Son's eyes, realizing the plight of the wedding couple: "They have no wine" (John 2:3). How embarrassing it could be for the couple! It would leave an indelible mark on their hearts.

God became man so we could "experience" His godly love with the taste of human affection. It is like what John said: "That which … we have heard, which we have seen with our eyes, which we have looked upon and touched with our hands, [concerns] the word of life" (1 John 1:1). We can now "imagine" our God: He walked the ways of the world. He felt weary, hungry, and thirsty. He was glad, angry, sad, afraid of suffering and death. He loved us and sympathized with us with a heart of flesh and blood.

He has bestowed grace upon grace. He gives us not only Himself but also His Mother. With a feminine, maternal, and meticulous love, she further manifests the love of God, enabling us to believe firmly and experience the company of God and His Mother at any stage of our lives and in any situation of our mental or spiritual states.

From the Cana wedding, we know how much Our Lady "meddles" with others' business. She has not given up either, right now in Heaven, and she cried out tirelessly in Lourdes and in Fátima that "they have no wine." "Sinners have made it hard for God to bear. Repent quickly and appease God's wrath! Prayer and penance are wines that please God."

Let us return to Cana. Jesus said to Mary, "Woman, what have you to do with me? My hour has not yet come" (John 2:4). No matter how difficult it is to comprehend this reply, Mary was certain that Jesus had granted her wish. She therefore asked the servers to get prepared. Jesus then performed His first miracle. His disciples began to believe in Him: their Lord was a great prophet who was compassionate and miraculous.

The prophet Isaiah said, "For as a young man marries a virgin, your Builder shall marry you; And as a bridegroom rejoices in his bride so shall your God rejoice in you." (62:5, NABRE). In the Gospel of Luke, the Pharisees asked Jesus why the disciples of John fast often, but His own disciples eat and drink. Jesus said that when the bridegroom is with them, the grooms should not fast (5:33–35). In this way, Jesus not only attended a wedding. He also revealed His identity as the Bridegroom.

Let the Christmas Octave and the Epiphany leave this stunning conclusion. God has taken human form and shared

His divinity with humanity. This union of God and man is more intimate and loving than any marriage. The Bridegroom first sacrificed Himself to win the Bride, rescuing her from the hand of the enemy and cleansing her with His own blood.

Let us now revisit the comforting words from chapter 16 of Ezekiel:

> On the day you were born ... no eye pitied you.... You were cast out on the open field, for you were abhorred. When I passed by you again ... I plighted my troth to you and entered into a covenant with you ... and you became mine. I decked you with ornaments.... I clothed you also with embroidered cloth.... You grew exceedingly beautiful, and came to regal estate. (vv. 4–5, 8, 11, 13)

"Where is he who has been born king of the Jews? For we have seen his star in the East, and have come to worship him" (Matt. 2:2).

I want to insist: Jesus is God; He is omnipresent and ubiquitous. The problem is that you usually don't recognize His presence. Saying that you come to Him today means that your meeting here strengthens your consciousness and confirms His presence. He has never left you, but you have lost Him, and now you have found Him.

You think you are looking for Him, but He is actually coming to welcome you.

The star stopped where the Baby was. "They saw the child with Mary his mother, and they fell down and worshiped him" (Matt. 2:11). The Magi from the East met Him two thousand years ago; today is a good day for you to meet Him.

"They saw the child, and they fell down and worshiped him." This Baby is the Son of God, who descended from Heaven and took on human nature. The Magi of the East knelt down to worship Him full of faith. It is said that these Magi studied astronomy and philosophy, and their worship of the newborn Jewish King must have had religious significance. In their hearts, this Baby must have had the status of God—the God who created all things and rules over mankind. We faithful in the New Testament are more blessed because we already know that this Baby will pay the ransom for us and save us from the slavery of sin. This lovely little Baby hides His divinity, puts aside His power, and is willing to be a vulnerable person, a poor person, a kind and humble person, not afraid that we could slander Him and even crucify Him. He wants to make a deal with us by taking our sinful humanity and sharing with us His divine eternal life.

"We have come to worship Him." Encountering the Creator and the Savior, the most natural reaction is, of course, to kneel down and worship.

The knee bones of the Chinese people seem to be very soft. In our culture, people tend to bend their knees in worship: before a judge, before an emperor, they have to bend their knees three times and kowtow three times each time. When we were young and paid New Year greetings to our parents, we also knelt on the ground and kowtowed.

On the other hand, some people seem to think that kneeling and kowtowing are detrimental to human dignity. Even in rituals and in front of the Holy Eucharist, there is no need to bend both knees; bending only one knee is enough. The early Church once forbade kneeling on Sundays because standing is the posture of the resurrected. The faithful today feel that it is more "cordial" to sit and talk to God.

The elderly faithful were very disapproving of the new practice. In the early 1980s, I accompanied a group of Italian friends on a trip to Beijing. One day, I went to the East Church to attend Mass. After receiving Holy Communion, I sat down and prayed to give thanks. An old lady came over to me and pulled my sleeve and said, "Kneel down!"

I smiled at her and said, "The rules of the Church now allow us to sit down after receiving Holy Communion. Don't worry."

After a while, she pulled my sleeve again and said sharply, "Kneel down!"

I said impatiently, "Granny, I am a priest. The rules of the Church are different from the past. It is allowed to sit and pray after receiving Holy Communion."

She squinted at me and said, "Are you a priest? I don't think you even look like a Catholic."

In fact, it is most natural to bend both knees and bow our heads to the ground to worship God. There are several occasions in the liturgy that require us not only to bend our knees but even to prostrate ourselves on the floor, such as at the beginning of the liturgy on the afternoon of Good Friday and when priests and bishops are consecrated. When sisters make perpetual vows, they even stretch out their hands as they prostrate themselves on the floor.

Pope Pius XII always gave people a very prestigious impression. When he was a cardinal, he went to Buenos Aires to preside over the Eucharistic Congress on behalf of the pope. His secretary entered the chapel of the Holy See nunciature at night. When the lights were turned on, he was shocked to find that Cardinal Pacelli had prostrated himself on the floor. The cardinal told him not to be surprised; he said that, being exalted to the sky all day long, at least he had to experience his own humility before God at night.

If we prostrate ourselves in ordinary prayer meetings, it will definitely cause surprise to others, but for some small groups to worship the Holy Eucharist, it is very meaningful to kneel down and bow our heads.

That star brought the Magi of the East to Bethlehem, which means "house of bread," and we faithful of the New Testament can fully understand what a meaningful coincidence this is. A grain of wheat fell into the good soil and died, from which a hundred new grains of wheat were born, ground up, and made into loaves. Jesus distributed it to the disciples and said: "This is my body, which will be sacrificed for you and be crucified on the Cross. Take it and eat it."

The Magi of the East worshipped the Baby in the manger; we worship Jesus in the Eucharist. His divinity is hidden in the manger, and in the Eucharist, His humanity is also hidden. This is the mystery of faith! When we participate in the wedding banquet of the Lamb, what we receive is the Bread of Life descended from Heaven. The Magi of the East took the Baby from the hands of the Holy Mother; from the hand of Mother Church, we receive the Holy Body of the Lord, the Savior predicted by the prophets and expected by all peoples.

Acknowledging that God is the Most High is also acknowledging that we belong to Him, so adoration and offering are, of course, inseparable. The Magi opened their treasury and offered gold, frankincense, and myrrh to the Baby. We all know the traditional interpretation: offering gold to honor Him as King and God, offering frankincense to recognize Him as the High Priest of the new covenant, offering myrrh to regard Him as the great Prophet who will pour out His blood to reconcile human beings with the Father in Heaven.

On the occasion of World Youth Day, Pope John Paul II gave an authoritative new explanation. He said that the gold you offer is your life, as you follow Him and respond to His call freely and out of love. The frankincense you offer is prayer and praise. The myrrh you offer is thanksgiving to the true God and true man who died on the Cross like a criminal for love of us.

Prayer and thanksgiving are not a problem, but are you afraid of dedicating your life? What does this remind you of? This reminds me of the rich young man in the Gospel.

The Gospel of Matthew (19:16–22, NABRE) records that a rich young man asked Jesus, "What good must I do to gain eternal life?" The biblical expert Cardinal Martini dissected the meaning of the entire dialogue in detail. The words *do* and *gain* highlight the characteristics of this young man as a businessman. He has done many transactions, and now he is planning to make a big deal. Let's see what good deeds Jesus would recommend to him and how much money He asked him to donate, so that he can buy the insurance for eternal life.

Jesus saw through his state of mind but did not reveal it. He answered him, "If you wish to enter into life, keep the commandments."

This answer is a bit too simple! What Israelite wouldn't know that? Of course the young man asked, "Which commandments?" As it should be, Jesus still took the second part of the Ten Commandments, which is the commandment to love your neighbor, as an answer. After hearing this, the young man asked, "All of these I have observed. What do I still lack?"

Among you, who dares to say to Jesus, "I keep all the commandments"? Was this young man too confident? It seemed that he was speaking the truth, and Jesus knew that he was speaking the truth too. The Gospel of Mark also says, "Jesus beheld him and loved him." So isn't keeping the commandments enough?

The young man could have said, "Lord, I thank You for affirming the direction of my life. From now on, I will continue to keep the commandments as before and enter into eternal life." But in fact, he felt that there was still something missing in his heart. He was a young man with visions, and he could not be satisfied by just keeping the commandments. Jesus was also blunt and solemnly replied, "If you wish to be perfect, go, sell what you have and give to [the] poor, and you will have treasure in heaven. Then come, follow me."

The phrase "if you wish to be perfect" was once interpreted as the religious life and the life of laypeople both. Many modern biblical scholars do not agree with this illustration, especially after the Second Vatican Council, as everyone has a better understanding that sanctification is the common mission of the faithful.

It is not good enough to be a good person. To be a saint is the only way to satisfy the desire in the depths of the heart. Jesus told the young man this truth that seemed to go beyond reason. It was a pity that he regretted asking the question he had to ask and that Jesus' answer was too much for him. Giving up everything, leaving everything—how could a person take such a risk? That is so unwise. What would others say? Would they think I'm crazy or suspect that something ugly is going on in my life that I can't tell anyone about? How can I live without property and reputation?

Matthew said that after the young man heard the words of Jesus, "he went away sad, for he had many possessions." Cardinal Martini said that, in fact, many things possessed him and made him a slave. His property, his reputation, and his status bound him.

It turns out that "blessed are the poor in spirit" means just this. The Virgin Mary is the most blessed because she deeply feels that she is God's handmaid, and she has nothing, so that the Mighty One has done great things for her.

Dear young people, you may say that I am not rich and I do not have the problems of the young man in the Gospel. Pope John Paul II once said: "Young people, you are all rich, your youthfulness is your wealth. Don't hold on to it; give it all to God. This is the gold that God is waiting for you to give out. Those who cherish life will lose it, but those who give their life can preserve it. Don't let your youthfulness be your stumbling block, hold your life in your hands and dedicate it to Him totally."

Worship and dedication are thorough actions that cannot be discounted. Young people, do you have the determination of "breaking the caldrons and sinking the boats"? Let us speak with full confidence: I am not a fool; you are not a fool; we are all smart young people. Let us do smart things. Let us worship Him and dedicate our youthfulness to Him!

"They departed to their own country by another way" (Matt. 2:12). The Magi got instructions from the angel in a dream not to go back and report to Herod, lest he kill the Baby, so they took another way and went back. "Another way" is a very good expression for a new life after worshipping the Savior.

For whoever meets the Savior, life cannot be the same as before. Let's go back to the rich young man in the Gospel. He must have had a hard time sleeping when he went home. He regretted asking for trouble in questioning Jesus, and he also regretted not having the courage to accept Jesus' call to follow Him. In the days to come, he might comfort himself: I could continue to be a good person, an honest person. Maybe he was determined to be more generous in helping others in the future, but he knew that he would never be the same again. The sadness would never leave him, and he knew that he had lost the unique opportunity of a lifetime.

The Magi's encounter with Jesus also changed their lives from what they had been before, but it was a turnaround worthy of rejoicing. John Paul II said that they would be worshippers of God all their lives, bearing witness in the world to the Savior they once worshipped in Bethlehem.

"Another way" symbolizes a transformation. The Magi were still themselves, but they were not what they used to be. They had found their true selves. They were still living in this world, but they no longer belonged to it.

In fact, the rich young man might have overlooked one sentence in Jesus' answer. Jesus said, "Sell all that you have and distribute it to the poor, and you will have a treasure in heaven." This young man who was used to doing business did not notice the terms of this transaction: use the wealth on the ground in exchange for the treasures in Heaven.

In Matthew's Gospel, Jesus went on to tell two small parables, but they are the key to success and failure.

A businessman with sharp eyes found a pearl one day. He knew it was a priceless treasure. Others didn't know the goods and didn't notice it. He immediately went home and sold everything and bought the pearl.

Jesus also said that the Kingdom of God is like a treasure buried in a field. Perhaps during a war, when the enemy invaded, someone hid all the precious things in the ground, but that person probably died, so no one knew the secret. Someone probably discovered the treasure while plowing a field, but it wasn't his field. According to the law, the treasure belonged to the owner of the field. The man who found the treasure immediately covered it up with dirt, went home, and sold everything to buy the field. Jesus said that the man "joyously" sold everything. His family thought he was crazy, and his neighbors advised him not to pay a high price for the infertile field, but he knew that there was a treasure in the ground.

When the Magi found the treasure, the sight of the Baby would remain in their memory forever, and the smile of the Holy Mother would support them all their lives as the apostles of the Jewish King.

If you really know the One you meet every time in the Eucharist is the Lord of Heaven and earth, the Savior of mankind, you must find another way when you go back. Of course, you are still you, but you can no longer be who you used to be. You still have to eat, sleep, make friends, and arrange entertainments, but your real interest will be to deepen your relationship with Him. You still have to study and work, but you are interested in asking only one question: "What does He want me to do?" The principles of economics encourage diversified investment to avoid risks, but we are not afraid of any risks, and we are determined to invest our whole life in Him.

Of course you still live in this world, but you no longer belong to it. After worshipping Him and dedicating your youthfulness to Him, you will be full of courage, be a different kind of person, not succumb to trends, not worship idols, and dare to be the salt of the earth and the light of the world.

"Live in the world as worshippers of God." What a meaningful perspective!

Some years ago, at a retreat held in a monastery at the place called Grand St. Bernard in the Alps, I gave lectures to seminarians and priests who came from China and were studying in Europe. The brothers of the monastery raised a breed of dogs called the Saint Bernard; the dogs carried small wine barrels tied around their necks and rescued lost climbers in the heavy snow. The motto of this monastery is very meaningful: *Christ adoré, Christ nourri*, which means "Christ adored, Christ nourished." We adore Christ in Eucharist; we serve Christ in our brothers.

Our last pope chose the name Benedict. Benedict was the founder of monastic life. The monks at that time preserved the culture of old Europe, civilized and educated the people who were still barbaric at that time, and laid a solid foundation for the new civilization in Europe.

The Second Vatican Council's Constitution on the Church says never to think that worshippers of God hate this world.

God sacrificed His Son for the love of this world. How can those who love God not love this world?

Maybe you will say, "We love this world, but this world doesn't welcome us. They don't like to hear us talk about Jesus. They believe that religion is out of date. They say that we need to rely on science and technology to transform the world and practically solve all problems."

Don't be afraid, young people; human beings are in a state of growth but are not mature yet, and their proud attitude is actually very ridiculous. What have science and technology achieved? Yes, many new things have been discovered, but the word *discovery* means to find. To find what? To find some mysteries that the Creator put in the universe? These are not really new things but only the codes that the Creator has hidden in nature.

Has anyone ever created a flower? Take a seed and look at it; peel it. Nothing special. But each seed has its code: a big tree grows from this seed, and a flower grows from that seed. Some flowers are red, and some are yellow, but there is neither red nor yellow in the seeds, neither red nor yellow in the soil.

Proud people are so ridiculous. Yet being ridiculous is the least we have to worry about—because this road that we walk is really quite *dangerous*. Man is like a naive teenager who discovers the mystery of God hidden in nature and thinks he has become God. He can exert power that was unimaginable before, but he can also use it to destroy himself. He already knows how to transform life and duplicate life, but the danger of this knowledge is unimaginable.

Let us live in the world as God's worshippers, influencing modern people with the attitude of worshipping God and awakening them not to worship the creatures and forsake the Creator. It is a pity that science and technology have promoted the culture of death at every turn. As worshippers of God, we promote the culture of life, the culture of love.

In the face of the war between Russia and Ukraine and the many precious lives robbed by COVID-19, we have asked many questions and heard many answers, but the only thing that can bring us peace is worshipping: to worship the Creator of the universe, the Lord of human history, Jesus Christ, who continues to suffer in every human being.

The Cross is a question: "Why did the innocent Jesus suffer such torture?" The Cross is also an answer: "Because God loves people so extravagently!"

After the Magi left, Herod still killed many innocent babies. The Magi could not have imagined it, but this did not make them doubt that they had worshipped the newborn

Jewish King. Herod's cruelty did not shake their faith; love would triumph.

Karl Marx said that people are too focused on understanding the world; let us transform the world! Faith allows us to understand the world, and this understanding gives us the courage and wisdom to transform the world and influence people's hearts!

Young people, Pope John Paul II called you the outguards of the dawn, depending on you to build a better tomorrow. Worshippers of God know how to build and not destroy. Worshippers of God love life, because God's plan is to give people life, abundant life, and "the glory of God is man fully alive."

Many people are waiting for salvation; many are reaching out their hands and wish someone would grasp them. You are not the Savior, but the Savior uses your hands. Grasp the hand of the Savior with one hand and stretch out the other hand to rescue people.

Sin brings death and suffering. People who do not worship God create much suffering. Let us worship the suffering Jesus. Let us alleviate the suffering of Jesus. People who do not worship God divide society, encourage discrimination, and promote collective selfishness. Let us bear witness to the love of Christ, care for society, and care for everyone in society, especially the vulnerable and the poor.

Around us, there are always people in situations more difficult than ours, people crying out for help, and people abandoned with no voice. Love will lead us to the manger like the star that appeared to the Magi, who adored Jesus, born in poverty.

In addition to material poverty, there is also spiritual poverty. Many people who live a wealthy life have lost the meaning of life. The poorest are, of course, those who have not yet known God. They search in the darkness and seek water in a dried-up stream.

The outguards of the dawn are evangelizers. Young people who have worshipped the Lord and dedicated themselves to the Lord would naturally become the witnesses of the Lord and would introduce Him to other young people. Pope John Paul said that only saints can successfully evangelize.

Is the mission of evangelization difficult? Certainly. Can we back down from this mission? No! The indifference of the residents in Bethlehem did not discourage the Magi, especially when they saw the Baby and His Mother; all the hardship of the journey and the trouble of searching and asking disappeared.

Neither the Bible nor tradition talks about where these Magi went to preach, but we know that a territory prepared by God for us is our magnificent motherland.

Meditation 23

The Baptism of the Lord

If we refer to the antiphon for the Magnificat of Epiphany's Second Vespers, we will understand that the feast of the Baptism is an extension of Epiphany. The antiphon says, "We celebrate a holy day adorned with three mysteries: this day the star led the Magi to the manger; this day wine was made from water at the wedding; this day Christ willed to be baptized in the Jordan by John in order to save us, alleluia."

The visit of the Magi, the wedding feast at Cana, and the baptism in the Jordan River—on these three occasions, God the Father revealed the Son to the world.

The baptism was originally a sinner's confession ceremony to ask for forgiveness, but it became a grand ceremony for Jesus to be canonized. "The heavens were opened [for him], and he saw the Spirit of God descending like a dove [and] alighting on him; and lo, a voice Heaven, saying, 'This is my beloved Son, with whom I am well pleased' " (Matt. 3:16–17). Before Jesus began His ministry, God the Father introduced Him to everyone: He was the great Prophet of the prophets, whom the heavenly Father had sent.

Peter's speech at Cornelius's house explained that this baptism was an anointing and consecration as well (see Acts 10:34–43, NABRE). God anointed Jesus with the Holy Spirit and with power. Anointing and consecration are, of course, inseparable from the mission. Peter said that God "proclaimed peace through Jesus Christ, who is Lord of all.... He went about doing good."

At the end of Christmas and the beginning of the ordinary period of the liturgical year, we will be led again by the Church to appreciate attentively what kind of Savior this Emmanuel who always accompanies us is: He is the "Servant of the Lord" and "the Suffering Servant." He did not come to judge but to proclaim grace. His power was in perseverance. He was neither discouraged nor disappointed. He opened the eyes of the blind and brought out of the dungeon the prisoners and those who dwelled in darkness (see Isa. 42:7).

The prophet Isaiah described Him this way: "He will not cry out, nor shout, nor make his voice heard in the street. A bruised reed he will not break, and a dimly burning wick he will not quench" (42:2–3). These words remind us of Isaiah 53:7: "Though harshly treated, he submitted and did not open his mouth; like a lamb led to slaughter or a sheep silent before shearers, he did not open his mouth." The prophet's words were clear. But when suffering came to Jesus, no one could remember the prophecies.

Those who walked by the Cross shook their heads and said in their hearts, "This man must have been a great sinner, that He should have endured such a fate." The chief priests, the scribes, and the elders further said, "Let [God] deliver him now if he wants him" (Matt. 27:43, NABRE).

Do we, today's faithful, understand God's plan better than those Jewish people did? What do we have in our minds when we ask God for an early reward of "triumph of the Holy Church"? The "triumph" that Jesus expected was: "Father, forgive them, they know not what they do" (Luke 23:34). The whole world was thus saved.

Stephen, before his death, also said, "Lord, do not hold this sin against them" (Acts 7:60). Saul, the young man who guarded the clothes of the Jews who stoned Stephen, was destined to be the Apostle to the Gentiles.

More than two thousand years ago, God the Father said to Jesus, when He returned to the shore after being baptized by John the Baptist in the Jordan River, "You are my beloved Son; with you I am well pleased" (Mark 1:11, NABRE). It was at that exact time that God opened the door of salvation to all mankind.

In the Great Jubilee Year 2000, television networks around the world broadcast footage of Pope John Paul II as he performed the Opening of the Holy Door. The climax of the ceremony was the deacon's booming chanting of the significance of the jubilee. (Unfortunately, the TV broadcast time was limited. It stopped as the deacon started to chant.) Through the deacon's words, the Church reminded us that the Holy Year is "a year acceptable to the Lord, a year of mercy and grace, a year of reconciliation and forgiveness, of salvation and peace."

Borrowing from Pope Leo the Great's homily for Christmas Day, the deacon said

> There is for all one common measure of joy because as our Lord, the destroyer of sin and death, finds none free from charge, so is He come to free us all. Let the

saint exult in that he draws near to victory. Let the sinner be glad in that he is invited to pardon. Let the Gentile take courage in that he is called to life.

Isaiah 55:1–11 emphasizes that by surrendering to the Lord, you will receive His mercy—because He is full of grace and love. He is the "water" by which we can quench our thirst at no cost. His words come down from Heaven like "rain and snow" and water the earth, making it fertile and fruitful. He wants to make an everlasting covenant with us.

All these have been fulfilled more abundantly in the New Testament. Three times in his Gospel, Mark proclaimed that "Jesus is the Son of God." When our Lord Jesus Christ was baptized and transfigured, it was proclaimed by a voice from Heaven; beneath the Cross, it was proclaimed by the mouth of the centurion. Precisely because Jesus is the "beloved Son" of God, He managed to accomplish the great work of reconciliation between God and mankind.

1 John 5:6 says, "This is the one who came through water and blood, Jesus Christ, not by water alone, but by water and blood." "Blood" reminds us that He is "the Lamb of God, who takes away the sin of the world." "Blood" reminds us of what He said before His Crucifixion: "There is a baptism

with which I must be baptized, and how great is my anguish until it is accomplished!" (Luke 12:50, NABRE).

The Church has marked December 26 to be the feast of St. Stephen, the first martyr, and December 28 to be the feast of the Holy Innocents, to commemorate the children of Israel killed by King Herod in his quest to find Baby Jesus. One can say that much blood had been spilled in front of Jesus' manger.

St. John stressed the "three that testify:" the Spirit, the water, and the blood. It is the Holy Spirit who makes water and blood work beyond their power. The Gospel of Matthew says, "the heavens were opened [for Him], and He saw the Spirit of God descending like a dove [and] alighting on Him." The descent of the Holy Spirit has made this baptism also an anointing.

We are all baptized in the Holy Spirit, who continues the work of Jesus Christ in us. To live in the Holy Spirit is "faith" and "love." St. John said, "The victory that conquers the world is our faith." He added, "We love the children of God when we love God" (1 John 5:2, 4, NABRE).

That our society is turning exceedingly secular is the reality we have to face, the challenge we have to accept, and it should also be a good opportunity for our faith to grow. People are closer to one another than ever before, yet our hearts have never been further apart. Selfishness has plunged humanity into a culture of death. Hopefully, in this new millennium, the culture of life will triumph.

Let us recall Pope Leo the Great's Christmas sermon once more, "Christian, acknowledge your dignity.... Recollect that you were rescued from the power of darkness and brought out into God's light and kingdom."

Meditation 24

The Presentation of the Lord

On the fortieth day after His birth, Baby Jesus was taken to the Temple to be consecrated to the Lord and redeemed with gifts. It was ostensibly a rite of slave redemption. But on this occasion, the Lord, the glorious King, "went into his temple." St. Luke repeatedly indicated that the prophet Malachi's prophecies were fulfilled (see Mal. 3:1). The Baby in the hands of the Holy Mother is "the powerful and mighty God, the invincible God." Simeon, an old man, took the Baby in his arms. Combining his identity as a prophet of the Old Testament and the New Testament, he praised and thanked God because he finally witnessed "a light for revelation to the Gentiles, and glory to thy people Israel" before his death (Luke 2:32). The elderly prophetess Anna also came to praise the Lord.

The order of Christmas in the liturgical year is supposed to be Advent, Christmas, and Epiphany. Still, we can see the baptism and the miracle of Cana as continuations of Epiphany. The feast of the Presentation of the Lord, forty days later, is more directly related to Christmas, which seems to be the true conclusion of the Christmas season. However, the conclusion of this Christmas order has already pointed to the Passover, foreshadowing it.

The Church traditionally values this day, although more emphasis was put on the role of the Holy Mother, calling the day "the Purification of Mary" or "the feast of Our Lady of Candelaria." The candlelight procession in the liturgy can be described as a prelude to the Resurrection candlelight procession, welcoming the coming of the Savior.

Passover, of course, contains suffering and resurrection. Simeon's prophecy unabashedly speaks of the fate of the Infant and His Mother: He will be a sign of contradiction—some will accept him; some will not—and a sword will pierce His Mother's heart (Luke 2:34–35). The Cross is the only way to victory. Without sacrifice, without suffering, there is no salvation.

BRINGING SALVATION TO THE WORLD

Meditation 25

How many still do not know of Jesus Christ?

In his Bull of Indiction of the Great Jubilee of the Year 2000 *Incarnationis Mysterium*, Pope John Paul II invites us to thank God with the opening address of the great Pauline Letter to the Ephesians: "Blessed be the God and Father of our Lord Jesus Christ ... even as he chose us in him.... He destined us in love to be his sons through Jesus Christ, according to the purpose of his will" (Eph. 1:3–5).

This is also exactly what the Second Reading for the feast of the Holy Mother of God emphasizes: "But when the fullness of time had come, God sent his Son, born of a woman ... so that we might receive adoption. As proof that you are children, God sent the spirit of his Son into our hearts, crying out, 'Abba, Father!'" (Gal. 4:4–6, NABRE).

The Gospel says, "So they went in haste and found Mary and Joseph, and the infant lying in the manger" and "When eight days were completed for his circumcision, he was named Jesus" (Luke 2:16, 21, NABRE). Our Savior did take the form of man, and specifically the form of a fragile, defenseless infant. He would like us to take Him, through the hands of Mary and Joseph, so that we shall have nothing to fear. Jesus Christ revealed to us the merciful and loving face of our heavenly Father and brightened our path of life.

How many still do not know Jesus Christ? Plenty. How many who know of Him are yet unwilling to obey? Not an insignificant number either. But it is undeniable that "the light shines in the darkness, and the darkness has not overcome it," and "the Word became flesh and made his dwelling among us, and we saw his glory" (John 1:5, 14, NABRE).

Meditation 26

How can those who have no faith be loved by God?

On the surface, a terrible thing happened two thousand years ago. Joseph and his pregnant wife could not find an inn in which to stay in Bethlehem, and Mary placed the fragile newborn Baby in a manger. But faith tells us that the Baby is the King, the "Wonder-Counselor, God-Hero, Father-Forever, Prince of Peace," through whom God manifested His love (Isa. 9:5, NABRE).

How, then, can those who have no faith be loved by God?

They may not know how to pray, and they may not know how to appeal, but the Holy Spirit will express in their hearts an inexpressible sigh, which is their pain, their despair. That is a different kind of prayer. Perhaps God is waiting for us to pass on their prayers so that He may launch a drive of benevolence and mercy. He is Emmanuel, willing to be with humans and sinners.

Meditation 27

We need to be evangelists too

Jesus, born in Bethlehem, is the foundation of the Church's "Catholicity." When the Word assumed a human nature, He formed an indissoluble bond with everyone. He has given us the most complete and decisive revelation about the heavenly Father. On the Cross, by His loving obedience, He obtained for us the forgiveness of our sins. He built the Church through the apostles and gave her rich and graceful instruments. His salvation is for all, for everyone.

What reassuring news this is! We are to cry out to Jerusalem, "Arise! Shine, for your light has come!" (Isa. 60:1).

Some people worry that if we are too excited to announce that Jesus is the only Savior, we will offend friends of different faiths and religions. Can't they be saved if they don't know and don't follow Jesus?

To say that Jesus the only Savior is to say that His salvation is upon everyone, and only those who knowingly and deliberately reject Him will exclude themselves from Him.

According to the Dogmatic Constitution on the Church *Lumen Gentium*, regarding "those who through no fault of their own do not know the Gospel of Christ or His Church ... or those who have not yet arrived at an explicit knowledge of God": if, moved by grace, they allow themselves to live good lives through the dictates of conscience, "they will not be denied the helps necessary for salvation" for it is Jesus' grace that sustains their good deeds.[5]

The Pastoral Constitution *Gaudium et Spes* elaborates: "The Holy Spirit in a manner known only to God offers to every man the possibility of being associated with this paschal mystery."[6] God has His way, and He wishes all to be saved. How can we fail to be optimistic?

[5] Second Vatican Council, Dogmatic Constitution on the Church *Lumen Gentium* (November 21, 1964), no. 16.

[6] Second Vatican Council, Pastoral Constitution *Gaudium et Spes* (December 7, 1965), no. 22.

This optimistic truth has also led some people to draw the wrong conclusion. They decide that we therefore don't need to evangelize.

On the contrary, Epiphany reminds us that *everyone* needs to evangelize. We may not know how God saves everyone, but we do know that He wants to reveal Himself through us, wants everyone to know the whole revelation, and wants everyone to enjoy the full sacramental service. His command is to "be my witness … and to the ends of the earth" (see Acts 1:8). To evangelize is our duty, our right, and our glory.

Thank you to those evangelists from the West for bringing us to Jesus; now we have to be evangelists too. Are the "chief priests and the scribes of the people" indifferent? Let us not be discouraged. Did Herod panic; does he intend to kill us? Let us not be afraid. That newborn Baby is the ruler of eternal life!

Meditation 28

The gift of peace

"Glory to God in the highest, and on earth peace among men with whom he is pleased" (Luke 2:14). Every year, the angels bring this message to all the corners of the world where Christmas is celebrated. Peace is the most cherished treasure everyone seeks to defend, if it is possessed, or to search for if it is still beyond their grasp. Too many people are agonizing over the threat of war or terrorism; too many innocent people—especially women, children, and the elderly—are suffering from the consequences of war, famine, disease, embargoes, or loss of their homes or homelands.

When the media put before our eyes such daily tragedies, let us pray for peace, God's most precious gift. Peace is not only a promised gift but is also a duty, a mission to be achieved. At the end of his prayer, Zechariah, the father of John the Baptist, asked the Lord to "guide our feet into the way of peace" (Luke 1:79). Yes, it is a way, it is a journey, and it is a construction, the foundation of which is built on justice and love.

An unjust situation made stable by oppressive structures is not peace but a state of violence. The prophets of God try to awaken the consciences of people by destroying false peace in order to correct unjust situations.

How does one create peace? You cannot deny desperate people their right of self-defense. Sometimes force seems to be the only way to free oneself from slavery. But it is also dangerous. Violence tends to create violence and may grow out of control, perhaps creating new injustices.

We Christians prefer to preach the truth that is the solid foundation of a just and lasting peace. "Peace among men with whom he is pleased" (Luke 2:14). Every human being enjoys the favor of God. Everyone is precious in His eyes because we are all His children, and we are brothers and sisters in the family of God. And here, love comes into play, where simple justice acknowledges its limitations. In the family, nobody is considered a burden, nobody is declared a failure, and the weak—children, the elderly, the sick, and the prodigal son—are entitled to more love.

We are living through a difficult time in our history. Prosperity seems to be a distant memory. Let us not surrender to the situation but work together to improve it. There is a wise saying: "By sharing our difficulties, they become smaller; by sharing our joy, it grows." Try it, and give peace a chance!

It is Christmas, and we exchange gifts. But the best gift is surely the one brought by Jesus; it is Himself: "To us a child is born, to us a son given to us; and the government will be upon his shoulder, and his name will be called ... Prince of Peace" (Isa. 9:6).

The angels appeared and sang: "Glory to God in the highest, and on earth peace among men with whom he is pleased" (Luke 2:14). Jesus comes and brings us peace.

What, then, is the secret of peace? Pope Benedict XVI gave us the theme for the World Day of Peace 2006: "In Truth, Peace."

We may object that it is precisely because we insist on truth that there is disagreement. If we put aside the problem of truth, is it not easier to live in peace?

But if we renounce truth, then there is only personal opinion. This may seem to be an open-minded attitude, but there is also the dictatorship of relativism. If there is no objective truth, my opinion may reign supreme, and I may try to have everything my way.

This is pessimistic. Jesus' coming has freed us from pessimism. "In him was life, and the life was the light of men" (John 1:4). "We have beheld his glory, glory as of the only Son from the Father, full of grace and truth" (see John 1:14). The truth is that God loves us and has given His Son to us.

John Paul II, in his encyclical *Redemptor Hominis* (The Redeemer of Man), told us that God, while showing us His love in the Incarnation of His Son, has at the same time shown us the profound dignity of man, who is so important in His eyes that He sent His Son to redeem him.

By His Incarnation, Jesus has become one of us; in Him, we are all brothers and sisters. Even unbelievers can agree on universal brotherhood. The problem is that we can be tempted by greed for wealth or for power; then peace is no longer assured. Only if we truly accept this truth of universal brotherhood and live by it will there be lasting peace.

The new commandment is to love everyone, each and every last person, and to love them as oneself: not just giving alms, like scraps from the table, but letting everybody sit at the table and share the fruit of the common effort of the whole family of humankind.

Some may have doubts in hearing this controversial bishop preaching peace. I think what I am doing is always preaching gospel truth and the teaching of the Church by defending human rights. Because of the dignity of each person, the bishop is entitled to participate in the affairs of society and not leave the decision in the hands of the rich and the powerful; this is democracy.

Thanks to organizations like the World Trade Organization, globalization is causing marginalization of the poor. We Christians are standing at their side—fighting for a more equitable system to guarantee their survival.

THE MOTHER IN THE PLAN OF SALVATION

Meditation 29

Mary's *fiat*

Luke 1:26–38 speaks of the Annunciation.[7] The prophet Isaiah and John the Baptist had prepared us to meet Jesus, but it is finally through the Virgin Mary that God gave us His Son.

We can say that Our Lady has taught us to trust in God, to follow Jesus Christ, and to obey the Lord's commands. "I am the handmaid of the Lord. May it be done to me according to your word." Nothing helps us prepare for the Coming of Jesus more than this attitude of humility and obedience.

[7] Scripture quotations in this meditation are taken from the NABRE.

The greatness of Our Lady lies exactly in this: to do God's will. Of course, she was chosen as the Mother of God, and, as such, she was freed from Original Sin. These were great honors, freely given to her by God. Elizabeth said to her, "Blessed are you who believed that what was spoken to you by the Lord would be fulfilled" (Luke 1:45). When Jesus said, "My mother and my brothers are those who hear the word of God and act on it," He was pointing out the true greatness of the Virgin Mary.

The reply that Our Lady asked the angel to relay to God was a lifelong commitment, an unconditional devotion. She needed only to know that this was indeed the call from God, and she resolutely embarked on this journey of no return, a path of gorgeous roses and prickly thorns. What a joy it must be to bear the Son of God! But how could she help St. Joseph understand? The expected labor was fast approaching, yet they struggled to find a decent place to stay in Bethlehem.

All these encounters were but the beginning, until a razor-sharp blade pierced the heart of this loving Mother. Young brothers and sisters, would you be courageous enough to follow the example of Our Lady? God probably will not send an angel but, rather, will invite you in other ways. Do not be afraid to open the doors of your heart to let Him in!

The protagonist in Luke 1:26–38 is not the Virgin Mary, but Jesus Christ, the incarnated Son of God. Nathan the prophet proclaimed, "Your house and your kingdom are firm forever before me; your throne shall be firmly established forever" (2 Sam. 7:16). Of course, the prophet was talking about the throne of David, but God's plan was far beyond the prophet's understanding. The angel Gabriel said to Mary, "Behold, you will conceive in your womb and bear a son, and you shall name him Jesus. He will be great and will be called Son of the Most High ... and of His kingdom there will be no end." This truly fulfilled the prophecy of Nathan.

The birth of Jesus Christ in Bethlehem became a watershed moment in history, drawing a division in time: "before Christ" and "Anno Domini" (the year of the Lord). Jesus is the King of all ages and the Lord of all history that ever was and ever will be!

The angel Gabriel said, "The Lord God will give him the throne of David his father," insisting that Jesus was the "Son of David." This fact was naturally of utmost importance for the Jewish community in the early days of the Church, and it remains significant for us today. Bearing in mind that Jesus was the Son of David means remembering that God's salvation was a historical process that took place in a specific space and time. The birth of Jesus was not an abstract concept but a historical event of flesh and blood.

During the Special Assembly of the Synod of Bishops for Asia, we emphasized that Jesus was Asian, born and raised in Palestine, where Eastern and Western cultures converge. At that time, the regime of the Roman Empire brought Europe and Asia together with Roman and Greek cultures.

"To the only wise God, through Jesus Christ be glory forever and ever" (Rom. 16:27).

Meditation 30

The Visitation of Elizabeth

When the angel Gabriel told Mary that God had chosen her to be the Mother of the Son of God, he also said that her relative Elizabeth had conceived six months before. The Bible does not say that the angel instructed Mary to visit her relative. Why did Mary set out "with haste"? Traveling from Nazareth to the town of Judah, where Elizabeth lived, was a difficult journey. Why did she remain with Elizabeth about three months? Certainly, this was done out of love and was done to serve. Mary had become the Mother of God. Yet, she acted like her holy Son. She did not regard her exalted identity "something to be grasped." Rather, she emptied herself, "taking the form of a slave" (Phil. 2:6–7, NABRE). She humbled herself to serve her relative.

Elizabeth was surprised and cried out in a loud voice, "And why is this granted to me, that the mother of my Lord should come to me?" (Luke 1:43). Faithful generations after generations have seen in Mary the example of humility and charity. All status or positions in the world are nothing but service—active and selfless service.

It was not only Mary who set out to meet her relative. She carried in her womb the incarnated Son of God. It was the Savior, Jesus, still in His Mother's womb, who wanted to start His mission in haste, to share His grace. John the Baptist "leaped for joy" in the womb of Elizabeth, welcoming the coming of Christ (see CCC 523). Wherever Mary went, she brought Jesus there and thus also the grace of the Savior. She accepted the Savior and became an instrument of grace.

The daily liturgy for December 21 pairs Song of Songs 2:8–14 with Luke 1:39–45. Christ is like a lover. When spring comes, He comes "leaping upon the mountains, bounding over the hills" to see His lover. And His lover had looked anxiously for Him. When she found Him, she "held him and would not let him go" (see Song of Songs 3:1–4).

The description in Luke's Gospel (1:39–45) was based on chapter 6 of 2 Samuel. The Ark of the Lord remained in the house of Obededom the Gittite for three months, and the Lord blessed Obededom and all his household.

Similarly, when Jesus, in Mary's womb, entered the house of Zechariah, He blessed Elizabeth and John the Baptist. The Ark of the Covenant represented the Lord's presence and help. It is the Lord who brought victory to Israel. And the victory Jesus brought to us was decisive.

The prophet Micah said, "He shall take his place as shepherd by the strength of the LORD, by the majestic name of the LORD, his God" (5:3, NABRE). The psalmist said, "O Shepherd of Israel, lend an ear, you who guide Joseph like a flock! Seated upon the cherubim, shine forth.... Stir up your power, and come to save us." The psalmist addressed God as the one who has planted the stock with His right hand, asking God to "visit this vine" He has planted (80:1–2, 15–16, NABRE).

The Letter to the Hebrews (10:5–10, NABRE) points out that Jesus' sacrifice is better than "sacrifices and offerings, holocausts and sin offerings." What Jesus offered was His determination to do the Father's will: the Father made Him an incarnated human being, and He was determined to become entirely a human who accepts suffering and death. Through this offering of Jesus Christ, we "have been consecrated."

To prepare our hearts (and souls) to participate in the offering of Christmas, let us grow in our hearts the trust and obedience Jesus had for our heavenly Father.

Our many secular messianisms place our hope in materialistic affluence, technological advancement, and social organization. Yet the Savior we are waiting for is the holy Son of God, who trusted and obeyed the heavenly Father. He shall be our victory; "He shall be peace" (Mic. 5:4, NABRE).

Meditation 31

The Assumption of the Blessed Virgin Mary

The Chinese faithful attach great importance to the solemnity of the Assumption of the Blessed Virgin Mary and list it as one of the "four big feasts" (the other three are Christmas, Easter, and Pentecost). This view is very reasonable. We know that Jesus' Resurrection is the foundation of our Faith, and His Resurrection is the beginning of our resurrection. However, Jesus is the Son of God, after all, and it is only natural that the heavenly Father would not allow Jesus' body to decay. Yet the Holy Mother is purely a created being, our sister. The great thing that God did to her—lifting her, soul and body, into Heaven—is truly the firstfruits of Christ's salvation. It more effectively assures us that what God plans for us is life—a full life.

God is willing to give every person, every saved person, a glorious body that belongs to God. "For he must reign until he has put all his enemies under his feet. The last enemy to be destroyed is death" (1 Cor. 15:25–26). Death is the consequence of sin, but Christ overcame sin and death. This victory brings not only spiritual life but also physical salvation and even the liberation of the entire universe.

When Jesus ascended into Heaven, the angel told the disciples not to just stare at the sky, for Jesus would come down as He ascended into Heaven. The angel would also tell us today not to stare at the sky, for it is true that we should be happy to celebrate the Assumption of Our Lady, but it is more important to follow in her footsteps. Filled with the Holy Spirit, Elizabeth revealed to us the greatness of Our Lady: "Blessed is she who believed that there would be a fulfilment of what was spoken to her from the Lord" (Luke 1:45).

In explaining "the Profession of Faith," the *Catechism* introduces Abraham as "father of all who believe" (no. 146); Mary is "blessed [as] she who believed." The Holy Mother also mentioned Abraham in her canticle.[8] The whole hymn

[8] The Magnificat: Luke 1:46–55.

synthesizes the faith of the Old and the New Testaments. This is the most beautiful prayer, with which the Church praises God in its daily Vespers, following the Our Father.

In this prayer, the Holy Mother fully expresses the spirit of the "Lord's poor people" of the Old Testament and demonstrates the principle of the "blessed" and "childlike spirit" of the gospel. It shows that God is omnipotent and merciful. It is He who looks upon His humble handmaid; it is He who helps those who are humble and trust in Him. The proud exclude themselves from His promises. Mary is the crystallization of belief of the Old Testament, the daughter of the New Jerusalem prophesied by the prophets, and the symbol of the Church in the New Testament.

Biblical scholars said that when Luke the Evangelist described the visit of the Holy Mother to Elizabeth, he probably remembered the scene in chapter 6 of 2 Samuel that described the transporting of the Ark of the Covenant to the city of David. The Ark of the Covenant represents God's presence among the people of Israel. God protects them and leads them to victory.

The book of Revelation describes a violent struggle between good and evil. That great and strange sign represents the Church. This description can also apply to the Virgin, since she is a sign of the Church. She defeated the poisonous dragon, just like the woman predicted in Genesis to crush the head of the evil snake (see 3:15). This great battle is ongoing, but Christ's victory is assured. Trusting in God as His servants and handmaids, like Mary, will win for us complete triumph.

Article 149 of the *Catechism of the Catholic Church* says that throughout the life of the Holy Mother and "until her last ordeal (cf. Luke 2:35) when Jesus her son died on the cross, Mary's faith never wavered. She never ceased to believe in the fulfillment of God's word. And so the Church venerates in Mary the purest realization of faith."

The Passion of the Holy Mother has been triumphantly accomplished. Her glorious Assumption encourages us to keep our eyes on the goal and to move forward courageously.

Meditation 32

The Rosary

The prayers of the Rosary are simple and easy to learn. The repetition of its prayers helps to calm the soul. Once this peace has been restored to our souls, Our Lady will be able to lead us into a deep meditation of the mysteries of Jesus Christ.

At the start of the new millennium, the Holy Father John Paul II told us that we should constantly contemplate the life of Jesus. The Rosary is a very useful tool that allows us to do this. The Holy Father encouraged us to meditate not only on the traditional fifteen mysteries of the Rosary—Joyful, Sorrowful, and Glorious—but also on five new Mysteries of Light. These allow us to meditate on Jesus' life before the

Passion: Christ's baptism in the Jordan; the Wedding at Cana; the proclamation of the kingdom of God with Jesus' call to conversion; the Transfiguration; and the institution of the Eucharist. Through our contemplating these mysteries, Our Lady can help us to become more like her Son and acquire holiness.

The holiness of Christians is not individualistic but communitarian, and the most fundamental community is the family. The Holy Father himself insisted that we should protect the family, which is the fundamental cell of society, the cradle of life, and the greenhouse of Faith. He said, "A family united in the recitation of the Holy Rosary will be kept united in mutual love."

The bigger family of the Church, during difficult times in history, experienced the powerful help of Our Lady through the Holy Rosary. Such was the case in 1572, during the naval battle in Lepanto, and in 1682 in Vietnam, when Christians were freed from a siege after praying the Rosary. Then in 1814, Pope Pius VII was freed from Napoleon, thanks to the Rosary. The Church today also faces many challenges; there is a great confusion of moral ideas and worldly temptations, but victory is possible through the power of the Holy Rosary.

The Holy Father encourages us to pray the Rosary for peace in the world. Wars are still raging, and many live under the threat of terrorism. Such conflict creates countless innocent victims and an escalation of hatred. Only our heavenly Mother can obtain from her Risen Son a real peace for mankind that is based on justice.

Conclusion

The Lord has completed salvation

During Advent, especially in the last week, the Church prays to God more and more fervently with the "major antiphons":

O Wisdom of our God Most High,
guiding creation with power and love:
come to teach us the path of knowledge!

O Leader of the House of Israel,
giver of the Law to Moses on Sinai:
come to rescue us with your mighty power!

O Root of Jesse's stem,
sign of God's love for all his people:
come to save us without delay!

O Key of David,
opening the gates of God's eternal Kingdom:
come and free the prisoners of darkness!

O Radiant Dawn,
splendor of eternal light, sun of justice:
come and shine on those who dwell in darkness and in the shadow of death.

O King of all nations and keystone of the Church:
come and save man, whom you formed from the dust!

O Emmanuel, our King and Giver of Law:
come to save us, Lord our God!

Are these the prayers of prophets in the Old Testament? Yes! Have all these prayers been answered? Yes! Then why do we have to repeat them? Because only those who seek will find, only those who hunger and thirst will be satisfied, and only to those who open their hearts with hope will the Savior come.

The Savior has come to the world and has completed salvation. He handed salvation to the Church. In the liturgical cycle, the Church takes us through hope and repentance to welcome the Savior again. On this Christmas Eve, the Church, whether in a majestic basilica or in a simple chapel, delivers the same good news: "To us a child is born; to us a son is given; and the government will be upon his shoulder" (Isa. 9:6). "The grace of God has appeared for the salvation of all men" (Titus 2:11). "To you is born this day in the city of David a Savior, who is Christ the Lord" (Luke 2:11).

Appendix

Singing Advent and Christmas

Singing has made up an important part of my formation and my liturgical spirituality. I still know some of the melodies by heart, even though at times they are no longer in use in our communities. Naturally, Advent and Christmas hymns formed an important part of this practice.

I used to sing an Advent antiphon in Latin when I was young. It was nostalgic, and the lyrics were beautiful. The antiphon was *Roráte caéli désuper, et núbes plúant jústum* (Drop down dew, O heavens, from above; and the clouds will rain down the just one). There are four verses:

1. Do not be angry, O Lord, at our iniquities. Behold the city of Your Holy Ones is deserted; Sion is deserted, Jerusalem now is desolate. The house of Your blessing and Your glory, where our fathers praised You.
2. We have sinned and become like some loathsome thing. And we fall like all the leaves, and our iniquities blow us about as the wind: You have hidden Your face from us, and struck us with the hand of our iniquity.
3. See, O Lord, the affliction of Your people, and send the One whom You will send; send forth the Lamb, ruler of the earth from the rock in the desert to the mount of Your daughter Sion, so that He will remove the yoke of our captivity.
4. Be consoled, be consoled, my people: I will send your salvation quickly. Why are you consumed with grief, why renew your pain? I will save you, do not be afraid, for I am the Lord your God, the Holy One of Israel and your Redeemer.

I find this truly beautiful, rich in liturgical spirituality with much to say about Advent. This hymn, in effect, can be sung every Sunday of Advent and thus savored continually as it merits. I had the good fortune of memorizing this song as a child and of enjoying it later in my community. This Advent hymn was inspired by the words of the prophet Isaiah (45:8), who says, "Rorate, caeli, desuper, et nubes pluant justum; aperiatur terra, et germinet Salvatorem, et justitia oriatur simul: ego Dominus creavi eum." These verses are found in the Church's liturgy in various modes; for example, as the Introit of the Fourth Sunday of Advent. But at a certain point, they were organized into a type of hymn with a refrain in the first mode of Gregorian chant. The verses recall our need for conversion and seem to have an almost Lenten tone. Let us remember that Advent is also a time of conversion.

I learned this when I was in Shanghai, when I entered the Salesians at the age of twelve. The missionary fathers taught us Chinese boys what was obviously the song of the Church. There were many of us Chinese aspirants wanting to enter the Salesians. Those were the hard times during the war. Family life was not always easy, due to widespread poverty. In the Salesians, we had the fortune of guaranteed boarding with regular meals.

The beautiful Advent hymn "Conditor Alme Siderum" comes to mind. I have to say, I am more familiar with another text that is sung with the same melody, "En Clara Vox," sung in the final days before Christmas. The third verse is very beautiful: "Vergénte mundi véspere, uti sponsus de thálamo egréssus honestissima. Virginis matris cláusula." These beautiful words represent Christ, who comes into the world, in the night of the world, into the womb of the most chaste Virgin Mary, like a bridegroom from his nuptial chamber. These are words of great poetry and spirituality. I really like this hymn in its Latin version. The Chinese version I like a lot less, for a reason I would like to explain. As we well know, it is a syllabic song. In other words, every note corresponds to one syllable. But in the Latin original, there are words of more than one syllable, and so it is simpler to be guided by the accent of the word and insert it into the architecture of the sentence. In Chinese, every note is a character that corresponds to a word, and at times, the execution sounds very hammered. The Chinese translations of Gregorian chant are not always fitting. Gregorian chant must be performed in the original because it is widely known that Gregorian chant is intimately united to Latin. This element is very important to remember. We would sing from the *Liber Usualis* that came from Solesmes Abbey, although now there are editions that, in my opinion, do not respect enough the Gregorian prosody.

I entered the Salesian Fathers in Shanghai in 1944. My mother presented me to a saintly priest, Fr. Carlo Braga, today a Servant of God. He was truly a person of great spirituality who was to have a great influence on my vocation. I had the joy of his presence at my first Mass. Fr. Braga, among his various talents, had the gift of music. Therefore, he and the other Salesian fathers strongly encouraged the study of liturgical song. The liturgy was, in fact, very well prepared. In effect, only three years after my entrance into the Salesians, Pope Pius XII was to speak of the importance of Gregorian chant in his encyclical *Mediator Dei*:

> As regards music, let the clear and guiding norms of the Apostolic See be scrupulously observed. Gregorian chant, which the Roman Church considers her own as handed down from antiquity and kept under her close tutelage, is proposed to the faithful as belonging to them also. In certain parts of the liturgy the Church definitely prescribes it; it makes the celebration of the sacred mysteries not only more dignified and solemn but helps very much to increase the faith and devotion of the congregation. For this reason, Our predecessors of immortal memory, Pius X and Pius XI, decree—and We are happy to confirm with Our authority the norms laid down by them—that in seminaries and religious institutes, Gregorian chant

> be diligently and zealously promoted, and moreover that the old *Scholae Cantorum* be restored, at least in the principal churches. This has already been done with happy results in not a few places.[9]

Even in Shanghai, these norms were already in observance, though we sang not only in Gregorian but also in polyphony.

In Shanghai, we lived in a large house. There were aspirants, including myself, novices, students of philosophy and theology, among whom there were some missionaries. They sang Gregorian chant in a truly sublime manner. When some sang the solo parts, although there were two, they seemed truly a single voice: there was a perfect fusion.

Naturally, we studied Latin too, which was certainly a struggle for us; we shed many tears, you could say, but this enabled us to comprehend what we were singing and to savor the beauty. Although learning Latin might have seemed complicated, singing in Latin was, at any rate, simpler.

Our music teacher was truly a well-prepared musician and demanding too: Fr. Cesare Brianza (1918–1986), an Italian priest who was quite young at the time of my studies but who knew his stuff. He had been in China since 1935

[9] Pope Pius XII, encyclical *Mediator Dei* (November 20, 1947), no. 191.

and therefore knew the environment well. This talented Salesian priest found his place in Macao, where he would stay for thirty years and where he would be able to use his talents at the service of the local community—among other things, directing a boys choir that he would take in concert even outside Macao.

I entered the third year of aspirancy, but for the first of these years I had to study Latin and therefore began to sing only in my second year. I must confess that at a certain point I was sent out of the choir. I was certainly not tone-deaf, but my voice was a bit "strange," and it did not blend with the other voices in the way our instructor wanted. Therefore, I had to stop for a year. I was later invited by the instructor to return, and understood why. In fact, although my voice did not harmonize well with the others, I was very useful when they sang pieces in polyphony for the part of contralto, which, as masters know, is often the most difficult, being a musical expression subjected to the melody itself. I had a voice that was a bit strange, as I have said, but I was quite secure in that regard. Thus, in one way or another, I made myself useful. The instructor told me to sing softly, in the ears of the others, more a prompter than a choirboy.

In 1948, we were transferred to Hong Kong to continue our studies for priestly ordination. I remember that a bit of Gregorian chant was sung here too, in the cathedral. I remember the schola that was made up of lay chorists who were a bit "elderly." I do not know why, but in this regard, my mind turns to the singing of an antiphon, *Pacificus vocabitur*, in the eighth mode, sung for the feast of Christ the King.

In my religious community here in Hong Kong, we still sing in Gregorian chant at times. Once we had some weeks of formation and prayer for our fathers, some of whom were leaving as missionaries in Taiwan or in China, so we alternated times of prayer in Mandarin, Cantonese, English, and Latin. Obviously, Gregorian chant represented an important part of this.

As regards the period of Advent, there was also the song "Tota Pulchra" for the Immaculate Conception. We did not sing the antiphon in the first mode, probably more popular in Western countries, but, rather, the antiphon in the fifth mode composed in more recent times by Dom Joseph Pothier of the Solesmes Abbey—a beautiful and noble melody that stays always in my heart and memory.

Christmas was obviously a time of great joy. This dates back to our founder, St. John Bosco, who gave much attention to the novena in preparation for Christmas and its music. There was, for example, the fine invitatory *Regem venturum Dominum*, with the nice verse that began with

"Iucundare filia Sion, et exsulta satis filia Ierusalem." This is a truly wonderful song in which the full Christmas joy can be savored. Quite handsome also is the Introit for Christmas, *Puer natus est nobis*, with that opening with the interval in fifth mode that describes for us something that arises but also a sense of stability, of power, which is that of the Son of God, who came into the world to redeem us and to bring the salvation of God to the entire human race. It seems like a trumpet sounding that announces the great joy of the Christmas season.

It grieves me that this repertoire today has been partially abandoned. I understand the desire to favor the participation of the people, but both approaches could have been taken. Also, during my time as bishop of Hong Kong, I sought to do something to this effect, but I think I could have done more, because sacred music is an integral part of the liturgy and must be well cared for and well sung.

About the Author

Cardinal Joseph Zen, a native of China, served as the sixth bishop of Hong Kong. He was created cardinal in 2006 by Pope Benedict XVI with the intention of working for the Church in China.

Sophia Institute

Sophia Institute is a nonprofit institution that seeks to nurture the spiritual, moral, and cultural life of souls and to spread the gospel of Christ in conformity with the authentic teachings of the Roman Catholic Church.

Sophia Institute Press fulfills this mission by offering translations, reprints, and new publications that afford readers a rich source of the enduring wisdom of mankind.

Sophia Institute also operates the popular online resource CatholicExchange.com. *Catholic Exchange* provides world news from a Catholic perspective as well as daily devotionals and articles that will help readers to grow in holiness and live a life consistent with the teachings of the Church.

In 2013, Sophia Institute launched Sophia Institute for Teachers to renew and rebuild Catholic culture through service to Catholic education. With the goal of nurturing the spiritual, moral, and cultural life of souls, and an abiding respect for the role and work of teachers, we strive to provide materials and programs that are at once enlightening to the mind and ennobling to the heart; faithful and complete, as well as useful and practical.

Sophia Institute gratefully recognizes the Solidarity Association for preserving and encouraging the growth of our apostolate over the course of many years. Without their generous and timely support, this book would not be in your hands.

www.SophiaInstitute.com
www.CatholicExchange.com
www.SophiaInstituteforTeachers.org

Sophia Institute Press® is a registered trademark of Sophia Institute.
Sophia Institute is a tax-exempt institution as defined by the Internal Revenue Code, Section 501(c)(3). Tax ID 22-2548708.